The 200 Communication
Commandments

The 200 Communication Commandments

Practical Tips for Personal and Professional Situations

Doug Campbell

ROWMAN & LITTLEFIELD
Lanham • Boulder • New York • London

Published by Rowman & Littlefield
An imprint of The Rowman & Littlefield Publishing Group, Inc.
4501 Forbes Boulevard, Suite 200, Lanham, Maryland 20706
www.rowman.com

6 Tinworth Street, London SE11 5AL, United Kingdom

British Library Cataloguing in Publication Information Available

Library of Congress Cataloging-in-Publication Data

Names: Campbell, Doug, 1972- author.
Title: The 200 communication commandments : practical tips for personal and
    professional situations / Doug Campbell.
Other titles: Two hundred communication commandments
Description: Lanham : Rowman & Littlefield, [2021].
Identifiers: LCCN 2021009175 (print) | LCCN 2021009176 (ebook) |
    ISBN 9781475860658 (cloth) | ISBN 9781475860665 (paperback) |
    ISBN 9781475860672 (epub)
Subjects: LCSH: Interpersonal communication. | Business communication.
Classification: LCC BF637.C45 C32 2021 (print) | LCC BF637.C45 (ebook) |
    DDC 153.6—dc23
LC record available at https://lccn.loc.gov/2021009175
LC ebook record available at https://lccn.loc.gov/2021009176

♾™ The paper used in this publication meets the minimum requirements of American
National Standard for Information Sciences—Permanence of Paper for Printed Library
Materials, ANSI/NISO Z39.48-1992.

This book is dedicated to my parents and grandparents, who supported me and gave me the opportunity to attend Furman University, where I was inspired to begin a lifelong study of communication and social skills.

Contents

Introduction

When I was eighteen years old and about to enter college, I had terrible communication skills. In fact, on a scale of 1 to 10, I was a 0. I was terrified of public speaking, uncomfortable in social situations of all kinds, and had no ability to talk to strangers. Whatever type of communication you could think of, I was pretty much terrible at it. My discomfort was so severe that I did not even go to my high school prom because it was too big of a social event for me to handle. And when my class had a graduation party, I remember sitting in the corner and hoping nobody would talk to me. I was the opposite of what you might call a "people person."

When I got to college, I quickly realized just how bad my communication skills really were. The mixer events that were set up for freshmen to mingle with each other made me realize how awkward I felt around people I did not know. In addition to that, the public speaking that was required in many of my classes was torture for me. After about a year of these kinds of struggles, it was clear to me that I needed to make an effort to improve—by a lot. I did not know what career I wanted to choose at that point, but I knew I would probably need better communication skills to succeed in just about any one that I decided to pursue.

When I was growing up, there were two areas of my life in which I did have confidence—school and sports. It was in both of these settings that I learned I had a gift for being able to both diagnose and improve my weaknesses, sometimes dramatically. So, it was not too much of a leap for me to try to tackle this next challenge—communication skills improvement.

The first step in my plan was to take a public speaking class. This was before the days of registering online, so I had to put a card into a box to sign up for it. It was so scary for me that I can still remember the moment almost thirty years ago when I dropped that card in the box with my schedule written on it. I can even picture the room where it happened. But I did it.

I was not in that class for long before I realized that it was possible for me to improve my speaking ability and comfort. It was still scary and stressful, but after a while I even enjoyed doing it! That experience really gave me hope, and inspired me to begin a lifelong study of communication skills.

The natural next step after my study of public speaking was a less formal exploration of social skills, so that is what I did. I began to get more and more bold, trying to figure out how to improve in social situations in the same way I had done with public speaking. This was a bumpier process, probably because I had teachers to help me when I was studying public speaking. For social skills, though, I was trying to figure it all out on my own. This led to some awkward and sometimes dramatic moments (especially in my dating life) as I tried to figure out the best ways to act in social situations. Just like with public speaking, I saw significant improvement. My social skills improved so much so quickly that I actually think that I accelerated too quickly for me to handle well, like a teenager who grows so fast his coordination does not catch up until later. I will just say that I made plenty of mistakes.

After learning some lessons the hard way, I realized that general social success includes three areas—what you *Say* (the strategy of your words to achieve a goal), how you *Act* (your character, likability, behavior, etc.), and how much you *Worry* (your ability to overcome anxiety, your social comfort, and general thinking). This is what I call my SAW System for Social Success.

When you have a challenge that requires communication or social skills of some kind, you must be able to communicate in a way that can give you the best chance of succeeding (the S part of SAW). You will also need to be able to stay calm and overcome any anxiety you may have (the W part of SAW). Even if you can manage to accomplish both of those, no amount of success is worth it in the long run if you can't achieve it with integrity (the A part of SAW). If you accomplish one or two of these areas but not all three, you have not truly become a great communicator.

This is a book of 200 tips and a "DO" and "DON'T" associated with each one to help you improve the way you speak, act, and worry in social situations. I call them "Commandments" because I think they are that power-ful. The more of them you follow, the better your chances will be of finding success in whatever situation you find yourself.

My approach when writing this book was to ask myself the question, "If I had the opportunity to travel in time and coach my eighteen-year-old self about communication and social skills, what would I tell him?" And not only what I would tell him, but tell him with urgency.

Each tip will either connect to a SAW system category or share wisdom of some kind. Thirty-seven of the tips also include a section that I call "Story Time," where I either give a commentary from my point of view or tell a story from my personal life that corresponds to the given tip. These sections act as an aside from my usual perspective of speaking to my eighteen-year-old self and are meant to reveal my inspiration for the tip.

My interest in communication and social skills has become more than just a strategy for career advancement. It is an urgent study of personal develop-ment that began in my second year in college, and one that I continue to this day. I have learned and improved so much in these areas over the years that I now want to help others experience the same growth for themselves.

Now, more than twenty years after I dropped that card in the box to sign up for my first public speaking class, I decided to write this book for people who want to improve their own communication and social skills as I once did. Whether you are low on the scale like I was or already pretty good and just trying to get better, this book was written for you. It does not matter how awful or awesome your current skills are—there is always room for improvement.

With that perspective in mind, I have written these 200 tips (command-ments), addressing everything from public speaking to starting conversations with strangers and getting the most out of networking events. I tried to cover as much as I could to help you improve the way you think, look, and act in social situations of all kinds, even digital ones. The more you learn about interacting with others, the better chance you have of reaching your long-term goals.

Hopefully, you will find something in this book that will help you over-come your weaknesses in the situations that challenge you the most. You may agree with some of my ideas and you may disagree with some, and that's okay. Of course, the more of these tips you follow the better, but I am

such a strong believer in the value of communication and social skills that
I believe that even learning one new idea could have huge benefits in both
your personal and professional life. Communication skills are that important
and that powerful.

If I could do it, so can you.

Chapter 1

Social Comfort

Overcoming Social Anxiety

Communication and social skills will not be useful unless you can figure out how to avoid anxiety when you are around people. The good news is this is a skill that can be learned.

*TIP #1: Be you and don't apologize for it.

The best form of mental toughness is to be so secure about who you are that you have no fear of people disliking you.

DO: Try to figure out what your strengths, weaknesses, interests, and traits are.

DON'T: Stress out about the strengths, interests, and traits you do not have.

There are some things about ourselves that we just can't change. For instance, when you are fifty years old, it is clear that you either achieved or missed your chance to fulfill your dream of becoming a professional football player. That ship has sailed at that point. If you hate math, you are probably not going to be a rocket scientist, no matter how badly you wish you could. And that's okay. The best thing to do is figure out who you are, accept it, and then refuse to apologize for the outcome. Worrying about not being able to achieve or be something you are not cut out for is a waste of time.

Being yourself not only applies to your career choice, but it also applies to your personality, strengths, weakness, interests, and so on. You should never feel pressured to be like someone else, and you should never feel bad for being the way you are (as long as the way you are is not dishonorable in some way).

There is one important part about this advice—being unapologetic about who you are is NOT an excuse to be rude, arrogant, or mean to people. Hopefully, one of the goals for being you includes trying to have class and character. To be clear, this is not a license to be self-centered and insensitive. It is more about committing to being your real self and not having a fear of being disliked or unpopular.

If you think about it, being yourself is all you can really control anyway. It is impossible to make *everyone* like you no matter how hard you try, and that is true of everyone. So, just focus on the one thing you do have total power over—the ability to be authentically you. Once you accomplish that, you can be free to just let people decide for themselves if they like you or not without obsessing about their decision.

Story time: When I was in college, there was a speaker at our freshman orientation who made an impression on me that would change my life. I even took notes on a lot of what he said (something I would have never thought I would do for anyone as an eighteen-year-old). One of his points, in particular, affected me so much that it immediately became my mantra for life. He said, "There is nobody in the world who everyone likes. So, my attitude is, if you like me, thanks. If you don't, have a good damn day." This statement rocked my world. I had spent my life up to that point being incredibly concerned about what people thought of me. Taking a "whatever" kind of attitude about people not liking me completely went against my usual mindset. Instead of trying to make people approve of me and worrying about it when someone didn't, this guy was saying IT DID NOT MATTER. By making the point that there is nobody in the world everyone likes, he was basically saying the math of the situation is that you will never be 100 percent popular. So why worry about the percentage who don't like you? There is nothing you can do to change it anyway.

*TIP #2: Be authentic in all social situations.

If you are hoping for long-term, dependable social success, the worst thing you can do is try to act like someone you are not.

DO: Commit to being yourself when you are interacting with people.

DON'T: Fake it in some situations just because you think that gives you the best chance to be likable.

Being determined on being yourself and "doing you" as I discussed in tip #1 can be freeing. There is a lot less reason to be anxious when you do not have to worry about how you are supposed to act to win people's approval. Yes, you may be able to have some short-term wins if you fake it, but they will almost certainly not last. The brief victories you have may actually backfire on you eventually if you are exposed for being dishonest.

The best strategy for big-picture social success is to figure out who you really are and commit to being that person *in every situation*. You may have to remind yourself of this strategy regularly if social anxiety or lack of confidence is an issue for you, but that is to be expected. This strategy is not always easy or automatic, no matter how good you get at it. There are also more benefits to it than just an increase in likability. The purpose of it is to use the comfort you feel from committing to being yourself as a path to confidence and anxiety busting. Now those are some outcomes that can dramatically improve your life.

Be careful: Remember that "doing you" does not mean it is an excuse to be rude or inappropriate. This is not a free license to just "let it fly" and go completely unfiltered. You will hurt a lot of feelings that way, not to mention that you will probably destroy relationships along the way. Committing to being authentic simply means that you are not afraid of being disliked or rejected for being who you are. The idea is to have peace about the fact that some people will like that and some won't no matter what you do. Once you realize that, you won't feel so much pressure to try to impress everyone.

*TIP #3: Keep a healthy perspective by having a "no agenda" mindset when talking to strangers.

If you have trouble with social anxiety, one way to overcome it is to totally release yourself from worrying about the outcomes of interactions.

DO: Have a long-term agenda when you talk to new people.

DON'T: Have a short-term agenda for every person you talk to.

Don't misunderstand, there is always some kind of agenda when you talk to someone. Maybe it is to make a friend or a business connection, or maybe the goal is to just be nice and spread some positive energy. This is not to say that you should never have a goal of any kind when you have a conversation. The "no agenda mindset" is more about the *short term*. If you are only obsessed with what you can get from every person you talk to, you will come across as pushy, insincere, and generally unlikable. Not only that, but you will find it hard to relax, too.

Your only goal when you are first talking to someone new should be nothing more than to *find out if there is a general connection*. Nothing more. This is true whether the interaction is personal or professional. Do not get so caught up in trying to reach your immediate goals that you forget to find out if the person is even interested in talking to you! It is kind of like trying to get a date. You would not want to get obsessed with trying to make someone go out with you when you don't even stop to find out if they even like you first. It is not good to have that kind of tunnel vision on your agenda no matter what you are trying to accomplish.

The more you can eliminate short-term agendas from your personal interactions, the easier you will find a way to be authentic. That is really the main goal you should be hoping to accomplish in social situations anyway.

*TIP #4: Count your blessings.

Counting your blessings can make you realize that the issue that is causing you so much stress and fear is relatively not that big of a deal in the long run.

DO: Remember how much good fortune you have had in your life.

DON'T: Assume everything will always go your way.

Overcoming social anxiety often requires a change of focus from a short-term to a bigger picture perspective. Living in the moment can take your attention off what is going right in your life in the big picture and make you focus on what is wrong (you can always find something to complain about if you look hard enough). But are things really as bad as they seem? Is your health good? Do you have family and friends? Do you have a job and a house? When we slow down to count our blessings, we often realize that our lives are actually pretty good overall.

Everyone knows that bad times will eventually come our way in some form or another. Maybe you or a loved one will have a health scare or tragedy. Maybe your business will fail. Maybe a friend will be disloyal to you. There are several things that can go wrong in our lives, and this is not saying that they are not a big deal. No matter how bad it gets, though, you still have had a tremendous amount of good fortune in your life. Just having the ability to read or hear this book is a blessing, for instance. There are many people who either do not have the means or ability to even do that. No matter what happens to you, you are still probably better off than many, many people in the world.

The next time you start feeling anxious about a situation that seems overwhelming, do not forget about all the good things you have going for you. This perspective can be a great way to reduce the anxiety you may be feeling.

*TIP #5: Talk to people wherever you go to build comfort in social situations.

One way to improve your communication and social skills is to be in the habit of talking to strangers throughout your day.

DO: Talk to people wherever you go.

DON'T: Size up everyone you meet to try to figure out if they are "worth" talking to before doing so.

If you are serious about meeting new people and improving your communication and social skills, you will work on them as much as possible. That means being open to practicing everywhere you find yourself through your day. These skills do not usually come automatically for most people, and you will not even completely learn them from just reading this book. It takes work.

There are some people who are strategic about whom they do and do not talk to. They are only friendly to others when they think they can get something from them. They see the attractive guy or girl or the successful businessperson, and they instantly start trying to win them over with charm and compliments. It's a self-serving and calculated style of social interaction, not to mention fake.

I think it is better to be a "never met a stranger" type of person. That means you don't strategize who you will and will not talk to. You are friendly to *everyone* you meet (when it is appropriate for the situation). The "never met a stranger" approach does not discriminate or leave people out for any reason. Every single person you interact with is worthy of your attention and positive energy.

Other than the benefits you get from making new contacts, the practice of talking to people wherever you go can also help drastically reduce your social anxiety. The more you talk to strangers casually, the easier it is during those times when you have to do it under pressure for some reason. With regular practice, you will no longer have to pump yourself up or figure out how to handle your anxiety when the time comes.

*TIP #6: Don't fear awkwardness.
   Awkward situations should not scare you so much that the fear of them cripples you.
   DO: Realize that awkward situations are a part of life and not usually that big of a deal.
   DON'T: Let the fear of awkwardness keep you from being social or trying new things.

Nobody likes being embarrassed. It is no fun. You should obviously have some awareness to avoid doing things that might make you look bad or awkward. That is just common sense. The point of this tip is to not let the fear of awkwardness *cripple* you from doing anything that might even seem a little awkward.
   The less you let embarrassment affect you, the more you will be able to reduce the fear of awkwardness. This is not to say that you have to be a total goofball or completely ignore general rules of normal behavior; just don't be so caught up in the fear of being judged that it keeps you from being yourself and doing what you want to do.
   The only way to 100 percent guarantee that you will never be in an awkward situation is to say and do *nothing*. Stay home. How boring would that be? I think life is more fun when we risk messing things up every now and then!
   I hear young people talking the most about the fear of awkwardness, so maybe it is just a matter of maturity and getting older. Whatever the cause of it is, don't let the possibility of awkwardness and short-term embarrassment stop you from living your life to the fullest.
   Be careful: Reducing the fear of awkwardness in your own life means you should also not be making fun of your friends if they do something embarrassing. Build each other up so that awkwardness is something to look back on and laugh at and not feel bad about.

*TIP #7: Get enough sleep.
   Sleeping better and more often is an underrated success strategy.
   DO: Go to bed early enough so you do not need an alarm.

DON'T: Think that sacrificing sleep so you can work harder is some kind of badge of honor.

So what does getting enough sleep have to do with overcoming social anxiety? That's simple—being well rested helps us stay calm, think more clearly, be more confident, and generally be at our best. Not getting enough rest has the opposite effect, so it would be wise to try to figure out how to avoid things that prevent us from getting the rest we need.

Sacrificing sleep may be necessary sometimes if you have no choice in the short term, but making it a habit is a bad idea. Some people may try to make you believe that staying up late is what successful people do, but don't believe them. The idea that sacrificing sleep is a necessary success strategy is a myth. Protect the amount and quality of sleep you are getting as if there is money, health, and happiness riding on it. Because there is.

*TIP #8: Do not worry about things that are beyond your control.

Worrying of any kind is unproductive, but it is a total waste of time and stress to do it about things we have no power over.

DO: Try your best when you can affect the outcome.

DON'T: Waste time worrying about things you have no influence over.

For such a simple piece of advice, it sure can be difficult to do. The logic makes sense, though. There will be things in life we have the power to change, and things we have no power whatsoever to influence. The outcomes that are beyond our control should not concern us.

This idea has applications for anxiety in general, but it applies specifically to social anxiety as well. One of the reasons that people can get so stressed out in social situations is the fear of things that they have no control over—like "what if someone doesn't like me?," "what if I embarrass myself?," "what if I fail?," and so on. You may have some influence over those things, but at some point you just have to try your best and let go of the outcome. The more you realize that it is pointless to be worried about things you don't control, the closer you will be to overcoming anxiety in social situations.

*TIP #9: Coach yourself during times of anxiety.

When you are facing a social situation that causes you anxiety, there is often no one to rely on but yourself. Don't worry, though. There are ways to overcome your fears and handle these stressful times.

DO: Prepare a few self-talk phrases for the times you feel anxiety coming on.

DON'T: Try to handle your anxiety in the moment without a plan.

If you have ever had issues with anxiety, chances are that you will never completely eliminate those problems. The good news is that it may still be possible to dramatically reduce it. One way that you may be able to do that is by preparing some anxiety-busting strategies ahead of time. In other words, instead of just trying to react in the moment, you can repeat some anxiety-busting phrases to yourself to get your mind in a good place.

The next time you know you will have to face a situation that usually causes you anxiety, try to make a list of three or four phrases that you think would help you and memorizing them. That way you can be ready to handle your nervousness if and when it comes. It may be an uplifting phrase like "act confident," "be at peace," or "you got this." It may be a Bible verse, or some other famous motivational saying. The actual phrase you choose is up to you. Just be sure you have *something* ready to go to.

You may also want to prepare different sayings for different situations. There may be some settings that make you more nervous and uncomfortable than others. When you have an actionable strategy prepared for the times when anxiety strikes, you don't have to feel so helpless. You anticipate the problem, and you know what you are going to try to do to handle it.

Also, if you try some phrases that don't work well for you, there is nothing wrong with trying something else next time. There is a lot of power in self-coaching, especially once you figure out a way that works best for you.

Story time: I once heard a basketball player being interviewed after a March Madness game where he had hit free throws in the final seconds to win it. They asked him what he was thinking as he was shooting the shots, and I loved his response. He said he was just telling himself over and over again to "relax and focus." I think this strategy can work in just about any situation where there is a chance we might feel nervous. All you have to do is figure out a saying that focuses on what you are trying to achieve and repeat it to yourself as needed.

That should help you get your mind in a good place and push the negative thoughts away. It may sound simple, but sometimes the most basic strategies are the most effective.

*TIP #10: Do not think about the white elephant to try to overcome negative thoughts.

If you get nervous in social situations, you may be tempted to constantly remind yourself to *not* be nervous. This may seem like a good strategy, but focusing on the things you want to avoid will probably make things worse instead of better.

DO: Use positive self-coaching sayings.

DON'T: Tell yourself negatively focused phrases like "don't worry, don't stress, don't be nervous," and so on.

Sometimes the opposite of what seems logical is the best strategy to follow. It may make sense to tell yourself what you *should not* be thinking. There is one problem with that idea. The only thing that happens when you tell yourself *not* to think of something is that you actually do think of that thing! As the saying goes, if you tell yourself, "Don't think about the white elephant," you will in fact think about the white elephant.

Whatever you intentionally think about is what is going to be on your mind. So, keep your thoughts goal-oriented and use positive self-coaching phrases like the ones that were recommended in tip #9 (coach yourself during times of anxiety) and you will have a much better chance of putting those negative thoughts out of your head.

*TIP #11: Act confident (in reasonable amounts).

Being fake or inauthentic can make you look bad *unless* the thing you are faking is confidence.

DO: Remind yourself to be confident when you have low self-esteem in social situations.

DON'T: Overdo it.

The popular advice to "fake it till you make it" can really backfire on you if you aren't careful. There is a time when it can be the right move, though, and that is when confidence is what is being faked.

It is unrealistic to think we will always be confident in every situation. Most people feel unqualified, inexperienced, or just generally anxious every now and then. It's normal. Sometimes it is to our advantage to *appear* to be confident, though. If you are in a business situation, for instance, you may need to present yourself confidently so your clients feel good about working with you. You would also probably want to look confident in a job interview, obviously. When you are in these kinds of situations, there is nothing wrong with faking it a little. Just be sure you don't overdo it.

So what is confidence anyway? I think true confidence is simply being comfortable with being yourself - no matter what other people think. It is not some fake arrogance and acting as if you are Fonzie from *Happy Days* or James Dean in old movies. Being a truly confident person simply means you know yourself and like and accept who you are. When you have that much self-assurance, you will automatically look confident.

Before you get to that point, though, there is nothing wrong with faking it a little.

Be careful: Acting confident is great, but there is a point where it is possible to show TOO much confidence. You do not want to try so hard to look confident that you make a fool out of yourself by obviously overdoing it. Showing too much confidence can make you look silly and fake, so be sure when you go for that little extra swagger that you keep it under control.

*TIP #12: Overcome "intimidating person" anxiety by valuing everyone highly.

One area of public speaking that does not get as much attention as it should is the skill of talking to someone who is intimidating. This can cause more anxiety and discomfort for some people than having to give a speech to a large audience.

DO: Think of yourself as friends with whomever you are talking to without worrying about being liked back.

DON'T: Worry about who likes you or approves of you, no matter what they can do for you.

There are many reasons some people may intimidate you. Maybe they are famous, powerful, good-looking, or older. Maybe they remind you of an intimidating parent or teacher. Whatever the cause is for you, intimidation in one-on-one conversations can be a very real cause of anxiety.

Overcoming intimidation is not easy, but I do think it is possible to accomplish. The best strategy for overcoming intimidating people is to value everyone we talk to highly, no matter who they are. That way when you do have to talk to an intimidating person, you are already in the habit of having a positive mindset about everyone. They become no different than anyone else, so you don't have to change your approach with them.

This approach can work for speaking to intimidating audiences as well, but it is especially useful when talking to one person. It is human nature to want to be liked, but we should not let ourselves be obsessed with that desire. The less we care about the opinions of others about us, the more relaxed and comfortable we can be around anyone. When you value everyone highly, no matter how they react to you, you release the fear of being valued back.

*TIP #13: Stay calm under pressure.

Everyone has to deal with difficult situations. The people who are the most successful are able to stay calm when the pressure is high.

DO: Make it your goal to remain calm during stressful situations.

DON'T: Assume you can't learn how to do it.

Have you ever seen people who seem to be able to handle any situation with calmness, no matter how intense or crazy things get? There is just something about them that seems so mature, professional, and together. You may be one of these people too.

There will be times in your life when it would be totally reasonable for you to get upset or stressed out, and nobody would blame you if you did. Staying calm under those conditions really stands out, though. Being able to remain relaxed and under control when it seems like you have every right to freak out is a sign of real strength, maturity, and self-control.

This tip would not be included in this book if it was impossible to achieve. If you are the type of person who has trouble being calm during stressful situations, the first step to overcoming it is realizing that it *is* possible to do it. Once it sinks in that you have it in you to stay calm when the pressure is the highest, sometimes all it takes is just a simple reminder to yourself that you can do it.

*TIP #14: Do not overvalue the significance of stressful situations.

Most situations are not usually as big of a deal as we think they are.

DO: Always try to be at your best.

DON'T: Add stress to situations by thinking they are a bigger deal than they actually are.

The job interview, the date request, and even just general social settings can overwhelm us if we think they are a bigger deal than they deserve to be. Notice that this does not say to think of every situation as if it does not matter *at all*. Of course, there are some events in our lives that are extremely important. The point of this tip is to try not to *over-assess* their significance.

Yes, you should definitely want to try your best to be successful in every situation. Just keep in mind that life will still go on if it doesn't work out the way you want it to. Unless it is a life or death scenario, the sun will still come up tomorrow and there will be new opportunities.

Be careful: The times we think failure would be the end of the world are when we perform worse than usual because of the stress we create for ourselves.

> Story time: When I was in college, I used to get really nervous when I had to give presentations. I remember one year I was taking a class on persuasive speaking and we had to give a sales pitch as if we were selling something. My professor literally said, "Oh no!" at one point during my speech and even made fun of my topic. I was very embarrassed and got a bad grade on the assignment. The funny thing about it though was that it turned out to be one of my favorite, most useful classes. I learned that even when things do not go as planned, there will often be more chances to start fresh and recover from our mistakes.

*TIP #15: Don't rely on liquid courage to overcome social anxiety.

Drinking alcohol is NOT a smart way to improve your social comfort.

DO: Drink a limited amount of alcohol in social situations if that is something you enjoy doing.

DON'T: Rely on drinking to help you overcome anxiety.

If your strategy for overcoming nervousness is to drink alcohol to loosen up, you are asking for trouble. Yes, it might help you relax, but you are also risking the negative effect it could have on your behavior. Even being the slightest bit tipsy can make you look bad.

Drinking too much can make us look bad in many different ways. This is not meant to be some kind of morality statement; it is just a simple strategy. When you are drinking, there is always a chance that you will not be in total command of your behavior. Even losing your self-control a little is not good in professional settings.

Be careful: Even if drinking did make you act cooler in a Dr. Jekyll and Mr. Hyde kind of way, you still would not be able to keep it up once you stopped drinking. So even if drinking did help your social skills, you still can't win.

*TIP #16: If all else fails in your fight against social anxiety, act like you are playing a part in a play of someone who is not anxious.

Sometimes pretending like we are someone else can reduce our anxiety.

DO: As a last resort, pretend like you are playing the part of someone who is not nervous.

DON'T: Go too far and change your personality too drastically to do this.

Social anxiety can seem like an impossible thing to overcome. You may have read every book, listened to every podcast, and watched every video about it, and still not experienced much improvement. Sometimes it can take a while to make progress. So, what should you do if you still deal with this issue but have no choice but to be in social situations? The answer may be as simple as pretending like you are someone else.

Social anxiety can take a lot of forms. Sometimes it may be a mild annoyance, and sometimes it is caused by a deep psychological issue. Unless you have the extreme version of it, you may be able to trick your own mind in the short term by simply *telling yourself* that it is not a problem. This is not a long-term strategy by any means, but if you need an emergency solution in the moment, this trick might be helpful for you.

Be careful: This strategy is definitely not guaranteed to work, and it would not be the first thing I would try if I had anxiety issues. I am just suggesting it as something to have on your list of strategies as a last option to use if anxiety is a problem for you. This is obviously a short-term fix, but there is something about pretending that can free us from worry and self-doubt.

*TIP #17: Connect your mindset in situations where you have no anxiety to ones where you do.

One way to overcome anxiety is to figure out why you are comfortable in some settings and not in others, and use that information to your advantage.

DO: Try to think of a time when you don't have social anxiety and try to copy that mindset in situations where you do have anxiety.

DON'T: Assume you will never be able to lower your social anxiety in certain situations.

Once you understand why you feel better in some settings compared to others, you can try to transfer that mindset during the times you aren't comfortable.

Social anxiety is not some blanket condition that we either have or do not have in all situations. If you thought about it, you would probably find a reason that you have less anxiety in some situations than others. For instance, maybe you are nervous when you have to speak in front of large groups but totally comfortable one-on-one. Or vice versa.

Once you discover what it is that makes you nervous in some cases but not in others, you may begin to figure out how to use that information to be comfortable in *all* situations. You may even be able to overcome your fears during those times that you thought you would never be able to handle.

Story time: During my time helping people solve their communication problems, I have noticed that many people have at least one social situation where they are uncomfortable and at least one where they feel comfortable. It was actually a surprise to me when I first discovered this. If you struggle with anxiety, you can use this tendency to your advantage to at least lower the number of situations that bother you.

Chapter 2

Likability

Communication skills are not just about getting people to do what you want them to do. Sometimes the biggest benefit you can get from these skills is likability.

*TIP #18: Be positive.

If you could make one change to try to be more likable, this should be it. Nobody likes people who are negative all the time.

DO: Focus on the positive when you are interacting with people.

DON'T: Complain about everything you don't like.

Being positive is not about being fake or unrealistic; it is about having a mindset of optimism, contentment, and gratitude. It also means keeping your complaints to yourself unless you have a productive reason for saying them.

We probably all know someone who finds something wrong with every situation. Maybe *you* are that person. This kind of attitude brings people down, and will probably eventually result in them not wanting to be around you anymore. Being regularly negative can be a hard habit to break, but it can and should be done.

Think about it, who would you rather spend time with—the person who has a positive outlook on life or the person who constantly complains? The answer seems obvious.

There are a million things we can find to complain about, if we look hard enough. This is not to say that there aren't valid reasons to be negative at times, just that we don't have to do it as a habit. It is a matter of perspective. You do not have to dwell on anything that you don't want to.

One thing that should be clarified about this tip—I am not saying you should be falsely positive and never complain about anything again. Being dishonest may be even worse than being negative. What I am suggesting is that you just do not make negativity your thing. You don't want it to be such a habit that people start to expect you to complain about something whenever they are around you! If your goal is to be more likable, it is time to cut back on your negative comments and complaining. Possibly by a lot.

*TIP #19: Don't be a sugar blower.

There is a point where it is possible to be *too* positive. This is called "sugar blowing."

DO: Look for opportunities to be positive when you can.

DON'T: Overdo it. Make sure your level of positivity is appropriate for the situation.

Sugar blowing simply means being fake or excessive with your positivity. When sugar blowers give compliments, they often do not really mean them (or at least not as dramatically as they say them). When they act like they are in the best mood of their lives, they, in fact, aren't. Honestly, what you are really doing when you behave this way is lying. You may not be *saying* things that are untrue, but you are acting insincerely. That is just as dishonest.

This advice is tip #18 (be positive) gone bad. Yes, I do recommend being a positive person, but too much positivity can make you unlikable. Just like eating a little candy can be fun; if you have too much of it, you will make yourself sick. Excessive positivity can have the same effect on others!

Be careful: I am not suggesting you shy away from being a positive person out of fear of going too far and looking like a sugar blower. That is not the point of this tip. Just be sure you are authentic and real with your positivity.

*TIP #20: Don't be a try-hard.

People who are try-hards often have good intentions, but they can still be very annoying.

DO: Make an effort to be kind to people.

DON'T: Be so over-the-top with kindness that you make it weird.

Trying too hard to make people like you is kind of like trying hard to hit a golf ball—at some point the more effort you make, the worse your results will be. In both situations, there is a sweet spot of just the right amount of effort that works best.

Try-hards are like hyper little puppies who do whatever they can to try to make you like them. They project a lack of confidence because they do not think they are worthy on their own, so they have to go out of their way to try really hard to gain your approval.

Be careful: Do not go too far the other way with this and not try at all to be likable. The point is to not be extreme about it. The best approach is to be yourself and try to be a good person and then be okay with people liking you or not.

*TIP #21: Do not get into arguments or heated debates over insignificant things.

If you are going to argue with people, at least make sure it is over something worthwhile.

DO: Have intense discussions about significant topics (in a respectful way).

DON'T: Debate and discuss minor things to the point that you are arguing, fighting, or insulting people.

The best-case scenario for debates and discussions is to have them without ever getting mad or losing your cool. Discussing things like politics, religion, business, and other serious topics can be interesting and fun. Even *those* debates should probably not get to the point of conflict, though. It is understandable how they could, but it is important that we make sure to stay respectful to people who disagree with us about things we feel strongly about.

It is bad enough to argue and get personal when discussing serious topics, but it is even worse when heated arguments happen about trivial things like sports, entertainment, where you are going out to eat that night, or whatever other minor thing you might be tempted to fight about. Not only does this make you look like a crazy person, but it can also damage relationships. It is just not worth it.

Be careful: If you realize you are the type of person who gets angered easily by people who disagree with you, you might want to try to stay away from discussing topics that you know could set you off. It would also be wise to

*avoid getting into debates with people whom you know who have a tendency
to get upset easily.*

*TIP #22: Try to avoid acting desperate in social situations.
    Desperation can make people lose respect for you. It's not a good look.
    DO: Connect your self-worth to being a good person.
    DON'T: Connect your self-worth to being liked by others.

Being desperate is nearly impossible to hide, in both personal and professional situations. People who beg for approval like that just have a vibe about
them that shows a lack of self-esteem and self-respect. It is hard to be taken
seriously when you do that.
    Not only will you make yourself look bad when you are desperate, but you
will not be able to have any peace either. It is hard to relax when your happiness depends on something out of your control, like people's opinions—that
may not even be based on truth anyway. Healthy self-esteem occurs when
your self-worth depends on what you think of yourself, not on what other
people think of you.

*TIP #23: Make kindness a habit.
    There is not enough kindness in the world. Some people are kind when
they think they can get something in return for their kindness, but very few
make it a way of life.
    DO: Make it your goal to be kind to *everyone* you meet.
    DON'T: Wait to be kind until you decide if you think a person is worth it.

Kindness with the hope of gain is nothing more than an attempt at a social
transaction. It is only truly authentic when you are kind without expecting
to be paid back for it. Imagine how much better the world would be if more
people regularly showed this kind of kindness to others.
    *Be careful: There will be people who do not appreciate your kindness or
return it back to you no matter how kind you are. Don't let that discourage
you from trying. Getting rewarded should not be your goal for being kind;
you should do it because it is the right thing to do. If your kindness turns out
to help you in some way, great. And if you end up getting no reward in any*

way for it, that is fine too. Let go of any expectations of being paid back when you are kind to people, and you will be happier in the long run.

*TIP #24: Don't brag.

Unless you are clearly trying to be funny, bragging can make you look like a jerk.

DO: Be confident.

DON'T: Tell people about how great you are.

Bragging makes you look insecure and needy, which is the opposite of what you are probably trying to achieve. People who are truly great at something should not feel a need to tell everyone about their greatness. It just shows. Not only that, but bragging makes you look obnoxious. Even if you *are* better than everyone else at something, should you really need to tell them about it to feel good about yourself?

There is nothing wrong with being proud of your accomplishments; just let your actions speak more for you than your words.

*TIP #25: Don't gossip.

Talking or writing negatively about people in public is not cool. This is something to put on the list of things to *never* do again.

DO: Be careful about what you say about people in public, even when your intentions are good.

DON'T: Say insulting things about people in public, especially if you are not sure if they are true.

Gossip may seem harmless and entertaining, but it can be very damaging to people. En.oxforddictionaries.com defines gossip as "casual or unconstrained conversation or reports about other people, typically involving details that are not confirmed as being true." This means that there are two parts to the worst kind of gossip—talking about other people and not being sure if what you are saying is actual fact.

There should probably be an even stricter standard for talking about people. Not saying things about people unless we know they are true should be obvious. An even better standard would be to stop spreading *true* information as well if there is a chance that it might make someone look bad.

Be careful: Some people do not even like GOOD things to be shared about them. Sometimes I think we might be better off if people just stopped talking about others at all.

> Story time: When I taught high school, I remember talking to some kids who did not want it to be made known when they did seemingly positive things, such as doing well on a test, making the honor roll, and so on. They thought it would make them look nerdy. This is why we should be careful about assuming that everyone thinks like we do. Even though most people probably do like being publicly praised, there is no guarantee that everyone likes it. Keep this in mind the next time you feel like talking about someone, even in a good way. I generally try not to name names at all unless I am positive they would like it.

*TIP #26: Don't be nosey.

The world is becoming less and less private. It seems like some people share everything they do online—and they expect everyone else to do the same. This is still not an excuse to push people to do it, though.

DO: Share whatever you want to share with people online and in person.

DON'T: Demand that other people share everything about themselves and what they are doing.

If you are someone who likes to share details about your life, that is your right, but that does not mean other people should be obligated to do the same. Don't push them. There is a fine line between showing interest in someone and being nosey.

Be careful: Do not push others to tell you about their lives, whether you want to know about a major event or something small like what they are doing for the weekend. Asking is one thing, but if you are being demanding or pushy, you are getting into the area of being obnoxious. You will be much more likable if you mind your own business.

*TIP #27: Don't be a busybody.

Being a busybody is high on the list of unlikable qualities.

DO: Mind your own business.

DON'T: Meddle.

Meddling in other people's business is one of the most annoying things you can do. According to dictionary.com, a busybody is "a person who pries into or meddles in the affairs of others." It is another level above my previous tip (don't be nosey) because a busybody not only tries to find out about your business, but they actually try to take action to influence your life in some way.

Be careful: Even if you are in a close relationship with someone, you should be careful not to be too much of a busybody with them. That kind of smothering behavior can be very annoying.

*TIP #28: Be obsessively dependable.

Most people are at least somewhat dependable. I think we should take it even further than that and be *obsessed* about it.

DO: Be committed to being someone people can count on.

DON'T: Be the kind of person who is dependable *some* of the time.

You should be so dependable that when you can't keep a commitment, people will be so surprised that they automatically assume that something out of your control must have happened. Your reputation for dependability should be that strong. There aren't many character traits to be known for that are better than that.

*TIP #29: Be careful about telling people, "I told you so."

"I told you so" is one of those phrases that can spark anger, even if it was not meant to be insulting or negative. Be very careful about how and when you use this phrase.

DO: Make sure your relationship is strong before telling someone, "I told you so."

DON'T: Value being right over potentially harming a relationship.

Being right is fun—there is no denying it. Just do not be so obsessed with being right and winning arguments that it hurts your relationships or potential ones. Sometimes it is best to value the relationship you have with people more than the joy of rubbing it in when you outsmarted them or knew something they didn't.

Be careful: I would avoid saying this phrase to people unless you are sure they know you are not a jerk because that is what you look like if you say these insulting words. Better yet, avoid saying it to anyone.

*TIP #30. Do not break plans with people casually.

Rescheduling plans with someone without having a great reason for doing so is extremely disrespectful.

DO: When you tell someone that you are going to do something, DO IT if at all possible.

DON'T: Break plans out of convenience.

Whether you have plans with a friend, a date, a business connection, or anyone else, they likely adjusted their day to include the appointment with you. When you break that plan without having a good reason, you are disrespecting the time they could have spent doing something else. By breaking a plan with people, you may really cause an inconvenience for them, so it should make sense to take this gift of their time seriously. Sometimes things that seem unimportant can make a big difference.

Be careful: Do not make plans with someone thinking that the plans are only "penciled in" and could be broken easily (unless you have made it clear from the beginning that you are doing so) if something better comes along. Treating these plans as though they are not set in stone without making this clear could make you look bad if you cancel them without having a good excuse.

*TIP #31: Be considerate of others (and say "thank you" when people are considerate of you).

If you notice an opportunity to do something thoughtful for people (like holding a door open, picking up something they dropped, etc.), then do it.

DO: Look for ways to do thoughtful things for strangers.

DON'T: Demand or expect other people to do thoughtful things for you.

If you want to be the type of person who makes a habit of showing kindness, you should try to be aware of potential opportunities to help the people around you. It takes a certain amount of social awareness to be able to accomplish this goal.

Most people appreciate it when others do something nice for them, even if it is something small. You will usually be thanked when you do, although that should not be the reason you do them. It should just be a matter of being a good person and treating people like you would like to be treated. And when somebody does do something considerate for you, though, be sure you thank them for it, of course!

Be careful: You may occasionally run across people who will not show you any gratitude or even acknowledge when you do something kind for them. Don't let that stop you. Yes, it is nice to be appreciated, but that should not be your motivation for doing it. Some people may even get a little HOSTILE about your act of kindness, as if it bothered them. This seldom happens, but if it does, just move on and don't let it bother you. That is their problem, not yours.

You are giving people too much power over your happiness and peace of mind if you expect them to be kind to you in the same way that you are kind to others. Being able to be good to people without expecting anything in return will save you a lot of grief and stress.

*TIP #32: Eliminate the phrase "shut up" from your life.

There are some phrases that can automatically spark anger, no matter what the intention or context of the situation is. "Shut up" is in this category.

DO: Never say "shut up" again.

DON'T: Say "shut up" when you are kidding around.

I know some people will disagree with me about this, but I think telling someone to "shut up" is a risky thing to do. There is just something about this phrase that comes across as disrespectful, no matter what the intent is.

It seems like there is almost a magical, negative, explosive power built into this phrase. It can mean a lot more to people than just "be quiet." No matter what the situation is or whom you are saying it to, telling somebody to "shut up" can often have unintended negative consequences. There is something about this phrase that has the power to flip a switch in people and make them extremely mad at you. It is hard to completely understand why this is true, but it is. That is why the best way to handle these kinds of potentially anger-sparking phrases is to avoid them completely.

Be careful: There are probably times when you could get away with telling someone to "shut up" with no problem, but why worry about trying to figure out when it is okay and not okay? I think you are better off just completely cutting it out of your life and avoiding the risk. It could cause you that much trouble.

> Story time: I knew a teacher who had a rule against saying "shut up" in her class. She called it "the S word." I never thought it was that big of a deal before I heard her talk about it as if it was a swear word, but it makes sense. I have seen people get upset when someone told them to "shut up" even when the words were not meant as an insult. There is just something about this phrase that can trigger anger. You are better off cutting it completely out of your life.

*TIP #33: Do not get mad at people who don't follow your advice after they ask for it.

When someone asks you for advice, you should think of your input as a suggestion, not a command.

DO: Be willing to give people advice if you think it might help them.

DON'T: Get upset if they do not follow your advice.

When people ask for your input about something, they are most likely just looking for ideas. They are in brainstorming mode. That means they have the right to disagree with you if they don't love your idea! If you get mad if they do not follow it, your intention was never to give advice but to give a command for them to obey. That is nothing but arrogance.

*TIP #34: Make a commitment to remembering and using people's names.

There is something about hearing our names that makes us feel good, so why not do our best to remember people's names when we meet them?

DO: Learn some tricks for remembering names.

DON'T: Underestimate the power of using the name of someone whom you do not know well.

For some reason, hearing our own names is like music to our ears. It is even better when someone who does not know us well remembers it. So, when you meet people for the first time, you should try as hard as you can to remember and use theirs.

This simple move can really help you make a stronger connection with people and increase your likeability! It may not seem significant, but it is. People remember when you remember.

If you are not good at remembering names, there are some popular tricks you can use for memorizing them. You can try things like connecting them to someone memorable, making up rhymes, thinking of a way to remember initials, and many other strategies. Whatever your memorization method is, it is important to do *something* to get better at this important skill. It starts with understanding how important it is and making the effort to improve. Do not just assume you are bad at remembering names and dismiss the idea of trying to get better at it.

*TIP #35: Keep your car clean.

Every now and then you may unexpectedly have to give someone a ride.

DO: Keep your car clean enough for guest passengers.

DON'T: Assume you will never need to give someone a ride without warning.

This tip falls in the "be prepared just in case" category. You never know when you might unexpectedly need to give a ride to a business associate, friend, or romantic interest. Make sure you are prepared so your cluttered car does not make you look bad if and when it happens.

*TIP #36: Have good posture.

This tip may sound like something an annoying relative would tell you, but I still think it's good advice to try to avoid slouching.

DO: Stand up straight.

DON'T: Think good posture is only for overly sophisticated people.

In addition to the health benefits of having good posture, there is also something about it that has a touch of class. It is probably not going to make or break your reputation, but these kinds of little things can make a difference.

Be careful: This is not something to obsess over or feel bad about if you don't do it 100 percent of the time. It is just one of those little things that can impact the way people perceive you.

*TIP #37: Don't "ghost" when you are not interested in talking to someone.

Sending someone the message that you don't want to associate with them anymore by ignoring them is not cool.

DO: Be honest if you do not want to talk, date, or communicate with someone anymore.

DON'T: Just disappear when you want to turn down an invitation or end all communication with someone.

According to dictionary.com, ghosting is "the practice of suddenly ending all contact with a person without explanation." For some reason, it seems like the more we have become dependent on technology, the more ghosting has become popular. Maybe we are becoming less and less polite as a culture. Or maybe we are so afraid of facing difficult situations that we flee from them instead of handling them with class. Who knows? It seems, though, that ghosting is on the rise.

Whether it is someone you have known for years or someone you just talked to once, ignoring them to show short-term or long-term disinterest is disrespectful. If you are trying to avoid conflict or an uncomfortable situation, you could consider the slightly less insulting method of turning them down a few times and hoping they get the message that you are not interested. Just don't vanish.

If you must "break up" or turn down someone (friend, business connection, romantic interest, etc.), hopefully, you will not have to go as far as bluntly telling the person that you are through with them. That may not be pretty, but just about anything is better than disappearing or ignoring someone to send a "not interested" message.

*TIP #38: Don't tell everyone about your problems (in person or online).

Complaining to people about your problems without asking for permission is inconsiderate and annoying.

DO: Share your problems with people in your close circle whom you trust.

DON'T: Share your problems publicly or with people you do not know well.

There is nothing wrong with telling your close friends and family about the problems and challenges you are facing. It is great to have people who you can confide in and lean on. The problem comes when you try to force your issues on people who have not given you permission to do so, whether online or in person.

People who dump their problems on everyone are making people be what I call "unwilling therapists." These people did not give you permission to dump your problems on them, and yet you force it on them anyway. It is not only inconsiderate but lame.

Be careful: Social media was a great invention for people who love to complain. They no longer have to wait to find someone in person willing to listen to them vent about everything that bothers them. Social media allows them to do it with large numbers of people all at once. Just because you have the opportunity to complain to huge numbers of people, though, that doesn't mean you should do it.

Do not assume that people are interested in your issues, especially people you do not know well. Be understanding enough to realize everybody may not want to hear about them.

*TIP #39: Be careful about using people's words against them.

Sometimes winning an argument with someone is not worth damaging a relationship (even if you are right). This is especially true if the strategy you use to win it is to throw someone's words back in their face.

DO: Be willing to participate in debates and discussions.

DON'T: Be a jerk about it by using people's words against them as a "gotcha."

When you use someone else's words against them, you better be sure that winning that debate is important enough to risk hurting the relationship. If it is not worth that gamble, it is best to avoid using this strategy.

It could be that there are times that you may think it actually *is* worth risking the relationship to try to win the argument. If that is the case, then so be it. Just realize what you are doing when you use this strategy.

*TIP #40: Do not try too hard to be cool.

The harder you try to look cool, the less cool you are.

DO: Have a little swagger.

DON'T: Have *too much* swagger.

Being truly "cool" does not mean that you strut around arrogantly like you own the world. True coolness is feeling comfortable in your own skin and acting calm and collected during stressful situations. Those things are REAL coolness. The problem comes when we think that coolness is really just an increase in swagger or attitude. Going too far with those things will not make you look good.

Be careful: Notice I said to have a LITTLE swagger. If you try to have too much of it you will look foolish. All you need is a hint of swagger—just enough to show you like yourself but not so much that you go overboard with it.

Story time: When I graduated from college, some of my family members said they enjoyed watching the ceremony because I looked like I was strutting across the stage to get my diploma. I did not even realize I was doing it! I cringed a little when they told me that because I do not ever want to look like I am trying to be cool. If my long strides or calm personality made me look that way, so be it. But going out of my way to try to look cool is not something I ever want to do.

*TIP #41: Be decisive.

There are not many things that make a person look weaker than a lack of decisiveness.

DO: Make decisions and stick to them unless you have a great reason for changing your mind.

DON'T: Go back and forth and continually ask other people what you should do for every little decision you make.

Don't get me wrong. I am not saying you should feel like you can never change your mind or never ask people for advice. Just try not to be in the habit of being wishy-washy.

Lack of decisiveness is often caused by fear. Fear of making a mistake, fear of failure, and fear of the opinions of others can paralyze us when it comes to making decisions. Once you learn how to face your fears and accept potential negative outcomes, it will be much easier to make choices without worrying about them so much.

*TIP #42: Do not be clingy with people you know during social situations.

The point of social events (especially business-related ones) is to mingle with different people. So, it should make sense that you should not just hover around a person who you know for the entire time.

DO: Talk to people you know when you go to social events.

DON'T: Hover around one person for the entire event.

At some point at social events you must be willing to step out on your own and talk to strangers, or at least different groups of people who you know. There is nothing wrong with sticking with your friends in these kinds of situations; just be sure you are not being a nuisance. Be considerate and realize that they may want to talk to people other than you. They may be too polite to tell you not to hang around them for the entire time, but you should still be aware that they may not want to hang out with you for the whole event.

*TIP #43: Slow down (speaking and movements).

Sometimes when we get nervous, we start doing things a little faster than we normally would. We may talk faster, breathe faster, move faster, and so on. Unless you are very good at hiding it, speeding up is usually not a good look.

DO: Learn some strategies to calm yourself down during stressful situations.

DON'T: Let yourself become too hyper when you get nervous.

It pays to look like you are under control, sometimes literally. Therefore, it is crucial that you figure out ways to relax when you need to. It is always better to have a plan instead of trying to react as it is happening.

Different strategies work for different people when it comes to calming down. You may want to try something like breathing deeply, memorizing a motivational quote, remembering times when you stayed calm under pressure, or something else that works well for you. There are several ways to do it.

When it comes to improving your communication and social skills, you should look at it from every detail and every angle you can think of. Every little thing could make a difference. Many times, you can accomplish this just by being intentional about slowing down your speaking and movements.

Be careful: Do not get so obsessed about this tip that you worry about it to the point of being stressed out. Just be aware of what you are doing so you can take steps to correct yourself if you need to.

*TIP #44: Overcome the fear of embarrassment.

It's no fun to be embarrassed, but at the same time it is also not the end of the world. Giving the fear of embarrassment too much power over you can keep you from being yourself and enjoying life.

DO: Do your best to live a life of character, integrity, and class and treat people well.

DON'T: Worry so much about people's opinions of you that you are crippled by it.

If you think about it, the feeling of embarrassment is 100 percent in your head. Nobody can make you feel embarrassed. The good news about that is that it means you have complete control over it. People have many different reasons for feeling embarrassed, but it usually comes from a fear of others' opinions of them.

Worrying about what people think of you can be a challenging thing to overcome, but it is important that you do. Being embarrassed may feel bad in the moment, but if you can keep it in the proper perspective, you will realize it is as big of a deal as it seems at first.

Be careful: I am not suggesting you go out of your way to act crazily and have no concern at all about the possibility of embarrassing yourself. It is still wise to be aware of how your actions come across to others. Just avoid being so fearful of looking bad that you are afraid to be yourself and live your life how you want to.

*TIP #45: Answer personal emails, texts, calls, and so on quickly.

The inconvenience of the effort that it takes to answer people quickly is worth the positive effect it will have on your relationship with them.

DO: Try to answer *ALL* messages (even from strangers) on the same day you receive them or at worst by the next day.

DON'T: Take it lightly when someone takes the time to get in touch with you.

Answering people quickly is an easy way to immediately improve your likability. Responding quickly not only shows respect, but it lets people know that you are dependable. This is not to say that answering people quickly will instantly make them love you by itself, but it is one piece of the puzzle that can help you look good.

The other good thing about answering people quickly is that it will separate you from (many) people who do not do it. You will look good in comparison, just by not being terrible at it.

I realize that it is not always possible to answer people immediately. We are all busy and messages can pile up on us. It is worth the trouble to try, though, and it is usually not that hard to do. If you want to be likable and establish a good reputation for yourself, answering people ASAP should be a priority.

Be careful: Do not think you have to answer with lightning speed every time someone contacts you. That is not the point of this advice. There is a difference between being fast and acting like you are instantly on call for people. That could wear you out. I do try to answer reasonably fast, but I usually don't answer people immediately unless there is an emergency or something urgent happening. Once you set the expectation that you will always answer in a few seconds, there is no going back. People will expect it from you. At that point, you are setting yourself up to disappoint people when you don't answer fast. Also, it should be obvious to not be someone who pushes others to answer YOU fast. Don't be part of the problem.

*TIP #46: Don't cry over spilled milk.

Crying over spilled milk means that you are stressing out about events that have already happened and cannot be changed. This is a waste of time and energy.

DO: Have a "whatever" attitude about inconveniences and misfortunes that are in the past and out of your control.

DON'T: Pitch a fit either outwardly or inwardly when something does not go your way that cannot be fixed.

Bad things happen sometimes. Some of these circumstances are in the category of minor inconveniences and some are major setbacks. No matter how

serious the bad event is, though, if you can't do anything to change it there is
no reasonable option but to roll with the punches and accept it. If the setback
was caused by a mistake that you made, learn from it and move on. Anything
else is adding unnecessary stress to your life.

*TIP #47: Treat people you meet as if they are already friends.

Instead of waiting to see what you think of people before you decide to
be kind to them, flip it around and act like you already like them from the
beginning.

DO: Imagine you already like people you meet.

DON'T: Worry about being liked back.

Talking to strangers can be a tough thing to do. You do not know how people
are going to react to you, so you must be prepared for anything. By imagining that you already like them ahead of time, you eliminate any reason to be
afraid of their reaction to you!

This is a great place to be mentally because you are in total control of how
you feel no matter how the interaction goes. You are taking full responsibility for your peace of mind during the interaction because your actions and
thinking are not dependent on the response you get. You are going to be kind
to them regardless of what they do (within reason, of course).

A lot of people take the opposite approach to this strategy—they are hesi-
tant and suspicious of people they meet until they find proof that the person
deserves their kindness and friendliness. The problem with that mindset is
that it leads you to come across as uptight and sometimes even rude. That is
obviously not the kind of first impression you want to give people.

Anxiety in social situations is often caused by a fear of not being liked.
Those fears are taken completely out of the equation with this approach.
Being liked by everyone you meet should not be the ultimate goal. Instead,
your objective should be to treat people well and look for connections. If
people don't like you or there is not a great connection, so be it. There is nothing wrong with moving on until you find people you get along with.

When you are already friends with someone, you are not going to be nervous, you are not trying to impress them, and you are not wondering if they
like you. That is why this way of thinking is effective. Having this mindset
when you talk to strangers helps give you the peace of mind of knowing there

is not much that can happen that can shake your confidence or comfort level. That is a great place to be mentally.

*TIP #48: Smile when you greet people.
Try to start every interaction with positive energy.
DO: Smile and act like you are happy to see people when you greet them.
DON'T: Overdo it and smile too big or insincerely.

This suggestion is similar to tip #47 (treat everyone you meet like they are already a friend), but instead of addressing people you are meeting for the first time, this advice includes the ones you already know. This means that you should start every interaction with positivity, whether they are with acquaintances or people who you have known for your whole life.

Be careful: I am not promoting insincerity with this tip as a strategy to manipulate people. It is simply a matter of giving yourself your best chance to be likable and connect well.

*TIP #49: Be careful who you tease and how.
Teasing people is a risky thing to do. It can show that you think of a person as a friend, but it can also make you look like a jerk if it is taken the wrong way.
DO: Tease people you like if you think they will understand that you do not mean it to be insulting.
DON'T: Tease *everyone* you know just because it is "your thing."

For some reason, we often tease the people we like the most. Maybe we are doing it for humor or maybe we do it to show a high level of comfort with certain people. It is true that teasing can be meant to be a compliment, though, even if it may not always seem that way.

Be careful: If you are the type of person who teases people you like, you have probably already discovered that some people appreciate it more than others. Some people may enjoy it and tease you back, but others may hate it. So, if teasing is something you like to do, at least try to figure out who can handle it and who can't. Otherwise, it could really backfire on you.

If you are not sure if a person is "teasable," it is probably wise to start out with something light and see how it is received. Do a little trial run with them before you go too far with them. If someone clearly does not appreciate your attempt to kid around, you should definitely not use this method of humor with this person. Don't force it.

*TIP #50: Do not automatically assume something is wrong with you if some people do not like you.

We give people so much power over our self-worth and self-confidence. It does not have to be that way.

DO: Your best to be a good person.

DON'T: Think it automatically means there is something wrong with you if someone does not like you.

There are usually one of two reasons why people may not like you:

1. You are not a likable person.
2. You are not their kind of person.

If number one is true, then you can do something about it. It is definitely possible to improve your character and likability. If number two is true, though, then there is no reason to worry about it! Sometimes two people just do not get along well for reasons that have nothing to do with character. That's just life. It is a *waste of time* to worry about something you can't change. Some people spend way too much energy worrying about things like this that they cannot control or change.

As long as you are trying to be a good person, the only thing you can do is let people decide if they like you or not. It is out of your hands at that point. Whether you are meeting people in personal or business situations, it is inevitable that some of them will click with you and some will not. You might as well just accept it and be glad for the good connections you find.

*TIP #51: Do not act as if you are in charge if you do not have the authority to be.

Do. Not. Be. Bossy. If. You. Do. Not. Have. Authority.

DO: Take charge if you are in a position of authority.

DON'T: Constantly tell people what to do if you are not in charge.

There are a lot of bossy people out there. Some are legitimately bossy if they are in a position of authority, but some just act like they are in charge even when they are not. The ones who do it without authority are Annoying with a capital "A."

Be careful: If you ever want to be disliked on purpose, a great way to do that is to start bossing people around when you are not in charge. Do not let this happen to you.

There is not to say that there is something wrong with making a suggestion or sharing your opinion with someone. I am not saying that you should walk around on eggshells, afraid to speak your mind. Just be sure you do not phrase your suggestions like you are *telling* people what to do instead of just giving them input.

*TIP #52: Be careful how you use sarcasm.

People tend to be sarcastic for one of two reasons—to be funny or to be insulting. If you are the type of person who has a "gift" for sarcasm, be sure you use it for humor only.

DO: Use sarcasm for humor if you are good at it.

DON'T: Use sarcasm as a verbal weapon.

Let's face it, some people like and "get" sarcasm and some do not. If you have a habit of being sarcastic in your daily conversations, you should be careful *how* you say it and to *whom* you say it. If you make a mistake with either of those two things, you could make some people very angry with you.

Be careful: Using sarcasm in written form is even riskier than doing it in person because there is more of a chance of being misunderstood. I would not use it when you are texting, emailing, and so on, unless you know the recipient really well. Even then, using sarcasm from a distance can still be a gamble. It can easily come across as just meanness if you can't observe the body language and tone being used along with it.

It is also a mistake to assume that people will know your sarcasm is meant as a joke. Even if your intentions were to be negative, people could still easily take it much worse than you meant. I am not saying you should stop being yourself and never be you if being sarcastic really fits our style; just realize that you are playing with fire when you do it.

*TIP #53: Never tell someone to "calm down."

Telling someone to "calm down" is one of those phrases that can spark anger no matter how good your intentions are. It makes sense to avoid saying it completely.

DO: Eliminate the phrase "calm down" from your vocabulary.

DON'T: Think it is okay to say it if you are kidding around or if you know someone well.

I am not exactly sure why this phrase can cause so much anger in people, but it does. And it seems to bring out an even more extreme reaction when it is said to a member of the opposite sex.

Telling someone to "calm down" can make people mad because it sounds like you are acting like an authority over them. Like it was said in tip #51: being bossy when you do not have authority can *really* make people angry. You can save yourself a lot of stress, conflict, and judgment in your business and personal relationships if you avoid saying phrases like this that can trigger anger.

Be careful: Do not make the mistake of thinking you know someone well enough that it would be no big deal to tell that person to calm down. Even friendly intent with a close friend or relative can get you in trouble with this phrase.

*TIP #54: Wash your hands after you go to the bathroom.

Some people pay close attention to see if you wash your hands in a public restroom, and it can be a big strike against you in their mind if you do not.

DO: Always wash your hands when you go to the bathroom in public.

DON'T: Ever be in such a rush that you skip washing after going to the restroom.

Even if you do not care about the sanitary reasons for washing your hands after you go to the bathroom, you should still do it to protect your reputation. This may sound random and unimportant, but I think it is a good strategy. I have heard negative comments from people many times about people who they saw who did not wash up.

If you do not wash your hands at home, as gross as that is, that is your business. When you do it in public, though, people are watching. You are communicating to them that you might not be as classy (or smart) as they thought you were. And they might be judging you for it.

*TIP #55: Don't be obsessively competitive.

Having a competitive spirit is not a bad character trait on its own. However, going too far with it can make you look at best like a jerk and at worst a little like a crazy person.

DO: Do whatever it takes (with good character) to win.

DON'T: Be a bad winner or loser or get too intensely competitive.

Some people are extremely competitive. This is a simple matter of misplaced priorities.

There is a point where too much competitive spirit can be excessive and annoying to others. Of course it is fun to win, but it is important to not take your competitiveness too far. Being *too* serious about winning and losing can make you look like a jerk.

It is difficult to say exactly how far is too far when it comes to crossing the line of being competitive, but sometimes you just have to use your common sense. It is okay to want to win; just don't let your competitive spirit overtake your sense of character and respect for others.

*TIP #56: Don't be an over-apologizer.

We all make mistakes, and we should be willing to apologize when we do. Just don't overdo it or you may make things worse than if you had not apologized at all.

DO: Apologize for your mistakes.

DON'T: Apologize excessively.

Have you ever known people who apologize repeatedly when they mess up? One apology is not enough for them, so they have to keep apologizing over and over again. They mean well, but after a while it gets annoying! Unless you do something *really* bad, one apology should do (maybe even if you did do something really bad). Much more than that and you just look like you are trying to kiss up. Whenever you make a mistake, you are better off just apologizing once and ending it there.

Chapter 3

Character Issues

Communication and skills are not just about being comfortable or even getting results. If you really want them to be great, there must be a third part of the puzzle—character.

INTEGRITY

*TIP #57: Be obsessed with doing what you say you are going to do.

It is an absolute must that you commit to keeping your word. It is that important.

DO: Follow through and try to do *everything* you say you are going to do.

DON'T: Be selective or casual about when you follow through.

This may be the most important tip in this book. Being in the habit of keeping our word is one of the most important qualities we can have in both personal and professional situations. This seems like common sense, doesn't it? And yet, so many people do not do it, at least not consistently.

There is a reason why this goes as far as using the word "*obsessed*" with keeping your word. Being true to your word is not only a matter of character, but it also builds trust, respect, and a reputation for dependability. You should be so committed to doing what you say you are going to do that you become known for it. This cannot be stressed enough. Lacking in any of these areas can seriously damage all types of relationships.

Let's face it. Sometimes unpredictable things will happen that make it impossible to keep your word. Maybe there was a huge traffic delay that stopped you from being on time or maybe you had a family emergency. Or maybe something completely unpredictable happened that totally blew up your day. These things can't be avoided. If it is in your power in any way, though, you need to make it a priority to make your word be dependable.

Some people are *pretty good* at keeping their word, but they still do it selectively. In other words, they only decide to follow through with their promises if something is convenient or important enough to them. This approach is better than nothing, but still not a high enough standard. If you commit to doing something, then you should go out of your way to do it, whether it is a big deal *or not* and no matter who you made the promise to. No exceptions.

For instance, when you tell people that you are going to meet them at a certain time, you should try your best to do it. If you say that you are going to email or call someone, do it. Use this rule in every area of your life. The more situations you apply it to, the better your reputation will be.

The good thing for you is that so few people committed to keeping their word at this high standard that you will stand out when you do it. It is a little sad that this basic matter of etiquette should make you different than most people, but it does. Take advantage of it and make yourself look good by being obsessed about keeping your word.

*TIP #58: Don't use NO ANSWER as your "NO" answer.

The practice of ignoring someone to send a message that you are not interested in doing something with them seems to be getting more popular these days. This is nothing short of bad manners.

DO: Always answer people who ask you to do something (in personal and professional situations).

DON'T: Let not answering count as your way to decline.

The logic behind this approach is that if someone does not answer you that you should be able to figure out that lack of response means "no." That may be true, but that does not make it any less rude.

This habit is so insulting because it leaves the person wondering what happened. Not only does it make them question why you declined, but it can also leave them doubting if you even saw their request in the first place if it was in written form. It is extremely inconsiderate to put someone in that position.

Sure, it is easier to avoid facing someone than face turning them down. Sometimes you just have to be a grown-up, though, and do the right thing despite the discomfort it might cause.

*TIP #59: Always choose the classy move.

In many situations, you will have an option to make one choice that is classier than other ones.

DO: Try to have class in all situations, even if it is not always the choice that will immediately help you the most.

DON'T: Show class only when you think there is a benefit for it.

We make tons of decisions every day. Some of them are minor, like deciding what to eat for lunch, and some are major, like what job to take. Every now and then, though, we will face a situation where one choice is more ethical than another one (although having class is not always a question of ethics). Those are the times that reveal which people have character and which ones don't.

If you are ever in doubt about a decision you have to make, whether it is big or small, you can't go wrong with choosing the classiest option. Even just *trying* to do this will put you ahead of most people.

*TIP #60: Do not be afraid to admit your mistakes.

Nobody is perfect, so there is no reason to feel bad about admitting when you mess up.

DO: Be willing to admit when you make a mistake.

DON'T: Feel like you have to admit *every* time you slip up.

If you think it would be appropriate to say you were wrong in a certain situation, admit it and move on. If you owe someone an apology, give them one. This is not to say that you should feel obligated to go public every single time you apologize; just be willing to do it if it seems appropriate. Protecting your reputation somehow by trying to act perfect all the time is not going to fool anybody, and it will only cause you stress trying to keep up to that standard.

MANNERS

*TIP #61: Be aware of other people's personal space.

This tip is not all that deep, but it is still important. Sometimes we get so wrapped up in ourselves or our devices that we lose track of what is going on around us.

DO: Be considerate of how close you are standing to other people.

DON'T: Be in your own world so much that you do not notice that your close proximity is making people uncomfortable.

Invading people's personal space can make them anywhere from slightly uncomfortable to extremely annoyed, so don't get too close if you can help it. A good rule of thumb for the correct amount of space to give people is about a foot or two away. Anything much closer than that can be awkward if you cross over that line. Always try to be considerate of how your actions may affect others.

*TIP #62: Learn from old people.

When you are young and cool, senior citizens may seem like the last people you want to be around. This is a major mistake. Elderly people often have wisdom that you can't find anywhere else, and they are usually more than happy to share it.

DO: Talk to elderly people when given the opportunity.

DON'T: Dismiss them as being unworthy of your time.

Not only is it the right thing to do to respect people from older generations, but it can also be beneficial. Improvements in technology in recent years have made it seem like we can find any information we want on the internet, but there are still some things that are better learned in person. Elderly people have likely already been through a lot of the same challenges you are facing, and they may have some great wisdom that they can share with you.

It is a compliment to ask people of any age for their advice or perspective. This is especially true of the elderly, so do not hesitate to talk to them when you can. Take advantage of opportunities you have to benefit from their influence.

Story time: When I was in college, I stayed with my grandparents for a couple of summers and I learned a lot from talking to them and being around them. If you are not lucky enough to have older family members who can share their wisdom with you, I highly recommend volunteering or finding another way to learn from these great resources.

*TIP #63: Show gratitude for compliments (even if you disagree with them).

When people say something complimentary to us, it is a gift that we should never take lightly.

DO: Acknowledge compliments, big or small.

DON'T: Ignore, brush off, or explain away compliments given to you.

There is no reason that showing gratitude should make you feel anxious. When someone compliments you, all you have to do is say "thank you" and leave it at that. It doesn't have to be anything fancy. There is no need to show false humility ramble on about why you disagree. Even worse, you should never ignore the compliment and act like it never happened. Yet many people do.

Be careful: I am usually sympathetic to people who are uncomfortable or unsure in social situations, but not in this case. Some people seem to think that if they try to explain why they do not really deserve compliments given to them that they are being humble. I understand the logic, but this is just not true. You are actually being insulting to the person who compliments you when you try to play it down or ignore it.

You do not have to make a big dramatic deal when someone gives you a compliment; just be sure you at least show some kind of appreciation. It does not have to be fancy or eloquent; just do it. A simple "thank you" will do just fine.

*TIP #64: Say "excuse me" if you bump into someone.

This is a simple rule of good manners that seems to be ignored way too often.

DO: Say "excuse me" when you bump into someone.

DON'T: Say nothing when you bump into someone.

It seems extremely rude when people accidentally walk into someone and do not say anything, and yet it seems to happen all the time. It is as if they are saying they are too good to be bothered by admitting they did anything wrong. How self-centered!

You do not have to do anything fancy when this happens; just say a simple "excuse me" and move on. Doing nothing and acting like it did not even happen makes you look arrogant and selfish. Be sure you always do the classy thing and apologize.

Story time: I remember when I was in my early teens and accidentally bumping into a guy at the mall. I told him, "Excuse me," and he laughed at me! I was a little embarrassed and confused at the time, but now I wonder what brought on that response. Was he from somewhere where manners were not taught or appreciated? Did he think I was a goody-two-shoes type of person for saying that? Who knows? My goal is to be considerate of others regardless of what they think about me for doing it. If they don't like it, so be it.

DOING GOOD

*TIP #65: Use your money to spread positivity.

There are a lot of ways that money can give people moments of joy. Sometimes it does not even take much.

DO: Be generous with your money in your day-to-day life.

DON'T: Be stingy, especially with small amounts of money.

The way people spend their money says a lot about them. Are you tight with every penny you have, or are you a generous person?

Yes, you can do a lot of good by donating large sums of money to your favorite charity or church. That is not the issue here, though. This is more about the way we use our spending money on a daily basis. A dollar here and there can often go a long way. For instance, you can give something to a homeless person who asks you or buy cookies from the Girl Scouts who have set up a table at your grocery store. A small amount of money has the power to make someone's day if you spend it wisely.

Be careful: Do not get so carried away with giving people money that you go broke yourself! Always be aware of how much you are giving to people. If you can afford it, though, give, give, give.

*TIP #66: Tip waitstaff one more dollar than what feels like the right amount.

One dollar probably means a lot more to your waiter or waitress than it does to you. It is an easy and relatively painless way to spread some positive energy.

DO: Tip waitstaff well when they do a good job.

DON'T: Feel obligated to tip waitstaff well when they do not do a good job.

This is not one of the deeper tips in this book, but it is still a good one. It is connected to tip #65 (use your money to spread positivity in your daily life).

There is just something that makes a waiter or waitress feel good about getting more than the minimum expected amount. It is validation that you did a good job. Think from the perspective of your waitstaff when you go out to eat and realize that even small amounts of money can make a big difference to them.

This is not meant to be an automatic rule, of course. You can still make sure the waiter or waitress gives you *some* reason to give them a little extra. I am also not suggesting you go above and beyond with your tip if they are rude to you or neglectful. If they do a reasonable job, though, try figuring out what you think an appropriate tip would be and then add one more dollar to it. Sometimes things that seem like small gestures to us can mean a lot to someone else.

Story time: When I first graduated from college, I used to wait tables to make ends meet. I must admit that I was terrible at it. For whatever reason, I just could not get the right vibe down to be successful at that job. I would pretty much always get around the traditional 10–15 percent for tips—meaning people rarely felt like giving me above and beyond the usual amount (like a lot of my fellow waiters and waitresses would often get). Here is the interesting part, though— when I got anything more than 15 percent, even if it was just one extra dollar, it was awesome! It was not just that the one dollar made that big of a difference in my life, there was just something about the gesture. I always try to remember how it felt to be a waiter when I am tipping someone now.

*TIP #67: Do random acts of kindness.

Doing kind things for people should be a habit for your daily life anyway, but it is even better when you do it unexpectedly.

DO: Look for opportunities to surprise people by doing something nice for them.

DON'T: Do not publicize or brag about it when you do.

Being kind when it is expected is a great thing to do. There are a lot of people who do not even go that far. But you reach a whole other level when you do something kind that is completely out of the blue, especially for someone you do not know.

You should be on the lookout for opportunities to do things that would surprise and delight people, like paying for the order of the car behind you at a fast-food restaurant, giving a huge tip to your waitress, or whatever other creative idea you can come up with to help someone. It doesn't have to be anything huge. Even small gestures of kindness can be meaningful to people. The possibilities are endless, especially if you can spare a little money. Not only is it a nice thing to do for people, but it can be fun too.

Also, when you are doing your random acts of kindness, you should try to do them anonymously if possible. Don't expect anything out of it for yourself other than the good feeling of making someone else happy. The reward of getting noticed for being kind should not be your motivation.

*TIP #68: Share what you learn about communication skills with others.

If you have learned something useful about communication skills that has helped you, do not keep it to yourself.

DO: Tell others what you know about communication skills if you think it could help them.

DON'T: Keep everything you learn to yourself to try to get an edge on everyone else.

Communication and social skills are hard to learn. They do not come naturally for most people. Whether you share your knowledge in person with people you know or go public with your wisdom online, you should not be shy about trying to help people with this important topic. Poor communication skills could be holding people back from success, happiness, and peace, and you could hold the key to help them get there. It would be a shame to keep something to yourself that might help others so much.

Story time: I did not originally plan to go public with my advice about public communication skills because it felt like a private issue. I started out just trying to help a few people I knew and planned to leave it at that. After thinking it through, though, I decided that these tips could make a big difference in a lot of people's lives, especially if their communication skills were as bad as mine once were. So, that is my motivation to write, speak, train, coach, and do whatever else I can to help people with this topic. If you have knowledge that could help make someone's life better, share it—even if it might be a little uncomfortable.

Chapter 4

Conversations

The ability to talk to people is obviously a key part of communication skills. You have to be able to start, continue, and end conversations with skill and comfort if you want to be able to connect well with others.

STARTING CONVERSATIONS

*TIP #69: Do not be afraid to talk to strangers.

Talking to people you do not know is one of the best things you can do to improve your communication skills.

DO: Talk to people wherever you go, when it is appropriate.

DON'T: Talk to strangers if you do not feel safe about it.

As children, we were often warned not to talk to strangers, and for good reason. When you are an adult, though, having conversations with people you do not know can be valuable. Having the "never met a stranger" mindset of being open and willing to talk to people wherever you go can help you in both your personal and professional lives.

You never know what a simple conversation with a stranger could lead to. You might make a new business connection, friend, or something else. None of those things will be possible, though, if you do not go out of your way to speak to people.

Is it possible that some strangers might be uninterested or even a little rude to you when you talk to them? Yes, it sure is. There is a good chance you will not get *anywhere* with most of the people you talk to. You never hear or see from them ever again, and that is okay. If you talk to enough people, though, eventually some of them will be great connections (that you would not have had otherwise). Learn to focus on the chance that something positive will happen instead of fearing the possibilities it might not work.

Be careful: I realize that there are some bad people out there. Obviously, you need to be smart about how you go about talking to strangers. If you are in a dark alley at 2 am, it might be a good idea to keep to yourself and not talk to anyone. However, in "normal" situations where you feel safe, by all means, you should look for opportunities to talk to people. Do not be so afraid of talking to someone dangerous that you totally avoid talking to new people at all.

The ability to talk to strangers successfully is extremely valuable. The more connections you have, the better it is. That is why there are multiple tips in this book about doing it successfully and comfortably. Being able to talk to people you do not know can improve your income, your social life, your love life, and much more. Do not let the fear of the unknown limit your chances of success and happiness.

*TIP #70: Memorize a few icebreaker phrases.

Some strategies for starting a conversation with strangers are better than others.

DO: Keep your icebreaker comments brief.

DON'T: Make them too dramatic or serious.

Starting a conversation with people we do not know can be intimidating. Are we being intrusive? Are we being rude? Maybe we are just causing an awkward situation? That is why it might be a good idea to think ahead and plan a few appropriate phrases you can say before you get into those situations.

If you break the ice too harshly and ungracefully, you run the risk of being disliked. If you do it smoothly, you at least have a chance that the conversation may go somewhere. The length of the resulting interaction is not important. What does matter is that you opened the door to a possible great connection and did it in a way that you can feel good about.

The key to a good icebreaker comment is that it does just what it claims to do—it gets people talking. That's it. You may continue discussing the topic you started, or you may break the ice in one direction and then quickly move on to something else. The topics don't really matter much. The important thing is that you tried to do *something* to get things going. The best icebreaker comments have power in their simplicity, so do not feel like you have to come up with anything fancy and impressive.

According to www.ldoceonline.com, breaking the ice means to "make people feel more friendly and willing to talk to each other." That is true, but there is even more to it than that. It is more like an invisible shield of ice that surrounds every stranger we see that stops people from talking to them. When you "break" this ice, you have now got past their shield and made it reasonable to talk to them. If you do this well, a meaningful conversation may occur.

An icebreaking comment is not meant to start a serious, heavy conversation. If it eventually leads to something deep, that's great, but you should not put pressure on yourself to *expect* that. If you are worried about not being able to start a long and interesting discussion, you will end up paralyzing yourself with overthinking and become afraid to talk to new people. All you have to do is make your comment and see what happens.

Be careful: I recommend that you memorize some icebreakers because you will not always have time to think on your feet. You may have only a few seconds to say anything before the moment passes, so it is much better to be ready and have something prepared to say ahead of time. Otherwise, you might miss out on opportunities to make a great connection.

Anyone can learn how to talk to strangers smoothly and comfortably. It begins with the right opening comment.

*TIP #71: Look for obvious reasons to make icebreaking comments to strangers.

Starting conversations with strangers does not have to be difficult. Like most social situations, it is just a matter of finding the right words.

DO: Comment on interesting or unusual things people are wearing, saying, or doing.

DON'T: Force it.

There are countless opportunities for you to start conversations with strangers. All it takes is one little opening for you to make a comment without making it look awkward. They are not hard to find if you pay attention.

One way to start conversations with icebreaking is to comment on the writing on t-shirts or other unusual things that people may have on. If the item is unusual or interesting enough, it will not be weird if you say something about it. If someone has a t-shirt with writing on it, they are expecting that people will be reading it. If they have purple hair, they realize that it might get attention. Therefore, you should not feel awkward or uncomfortable making a casual comment about other people's unusual items or apparel.

Another way to find opportunities to talk to people you do not know is by casually standing near groups of people and trying to "accidentally" overhear what they are talking about. If you hear something interesting, you can then casually throw in your two cents. Just be sure if you use this strategy that you do not make it too obvious. If you want to eavesdrop successfully, you have to be able to make your comment and then be willing to get in or out of the conversation quickly, depending on the response. Don't go out of your way too much to listen to other people's conversations unless they are loud and clearly not trying to be private.

Whatever style of icebreaker you choose to use, it should be extremely simple. If you aren't feeling creative, you could even just start out by saying something like "how are you" and see if how it is received. Casual is key.

Be careful: Make sure the things you are commenting on are legitimately out of the ordinary or unusual or you may cause an awkward situation. Commenting about something that does not really stand out will make you look like you are up to something. If you are going to make comments about things you overhear in peoples' conversations, make sure you keep the topics safe and casual. Avoid saying anything about someone's personal business or sensitive topics.

*TIP #72: Master the throwaway comment.

A throwaway comment is something you say when you want to try to break the ice with a stranger but are not concerned about it going anywhere after you make your comment.

DO: Practice and master your ability to make throwaway comments.

DON'T: Be afraid that your throwaway comments won't work.

Being able to use throwaway comments is one of the keys to talking to strangers well. When you want to talk to someone with the possibility of starting a conversation, it is best to start out with something quick and light. That way, you haven't invested too much of yourself in the conversation if it does not happen to work.

There are two things that can happen when you make a throwaway comment—either the stranger continues the conversation or it ends there. Since you are (hopefully) not worried about it either way, you are pretty much just throwing words out there and seeing what happens. If it works, it works. If it doesn't, it doesn't. It is not a big deal either way. This is really a no-lose situation if you think about it like this! When there is no possibility of failure, the only possible outcomes are success and neutral. That is a beautiful place to be mentally. Also, since you are able to be a lot more at ease about making these kinds of comments, the situation will of course become more relaxed and casual.

There are three types of throwaway comments that are most effective: (1) observational, (2) casual compliments, and (3) simple greetings.

1.) Observational throwaway comments. An observational throwaway comment is just what it sounds like—you are observing something that stands out. It can be something as simple as the weather or it can be a comment about something interesting that is happening around you. The possibilities are endless. To pull off this kind of throwaway comment, all you have to do is pay attention and look for something out of the ordinary to talk about.

2.) Casual compliment throwaway comments. The goal here is to say you like something about a person without going overboard.

    If you are not sure exactly what to compliment about, start by limiting your topics to more usual items of clothing like shoes, hats, jewelry, and so on, and not talk about anything too personal. Avoid compliments about body parts (no saying things like "you have pretty eyes"). And, of course, you should try to find something you *actually* do like, so you do not have to be insincere.

    Be careful: The last thing you want to do is look like you are trying to immediately hit on someone (even if that is your ultimate goal), so it is important to be VERY calm and casual when you make these kinds of compliments to strangers. You do not want to look like a threat in any way.

3.) Simple greeting throwaway comments. Believe it or not, sometimes saying something as simple as "How are you?" can be enough of an opening to start a conversation. Yes, it may also end with the other person saying "fine" and having it end right there. Or it may spark a long conversation. It is no big deal either way. Just be sure you are prepared to follow up with small talk if they do want to keep talking. If you are afraid of having to think on your feet to make compliments or observational comments, this simple greeting strategy is a great strategy.

*TIP #73: Be open to having strangers start conversations with you.

If you are going to be talking to strangers yourself, it makes sense that you should be open to people trying to do the same thing with you.

DO: Have a friendly and welcoming personality so people feel comfortable talking to you.

DON'T: Have a general attitude of avoiding talking to strangers.

There are a lot of scary people in the world. There is no doubt about it. But we can't let the fear of them stop us from meeting new people and talking to strangers. Do not be so afraid of the very small percentage of dangerous people out there that you close yourself off to talking to anyone at all. That includes trying not to communicate to people nonverbally that you don't want to be approached. It is best to avoid closed body language habits like avoiding eye contact, keeping your nose stuck in your phone, or wearing earbuds to put up a barrier to conversation when you are around people.

There are a lot of possible benefits from talking to strangers for both our personal and professional lives. Not only should we be willing to start conversations with new people, we should also be open to having others do the same to us. You never know what good could come out of it.

Story time: Someone I had just met told me one time that I was easy to approach because I had such an open vibe and posture. That was a great compliment! Since I work so hard at starting conversations with new people myself, I try to be equally open to people trying to do the same with me. That requires having a generally positive mindset as well as positive body language. It makes a difference.

*TIP #74: Wear unusual things that might inspire others to start a conversation with you.

Anything you can do to make it easier for strangers to start a conversation with you is a plus.

DO: Wear clothes or accessories that are out of the ordinary enough to inspire comments.

DON'T: Go overboard or wear things that do not fit your style.

Finding ways to start a conversation with people you do not know is not easy. If you follow the tips I give you in this section, you should be able to get pretty good at it. You can also make it easier for other people to start talking to *you* by wearing things that could inspire comments.

When you are wearing something that clearly stands out, you give people an easy reason to say something to you. Many of them probably would not speak to you at all without your help, but if you wear something interesting enough, they might do it.

Be careful: I am not suggesting you go crazy and put on outrageous or embarrassing things that you would not usually wear. Just choose clothes that stand out enough to make someone want to comment. This is also not something you have to do EVERY time you go out in public, just something for you to try every now and then.

You do not want conversations to seem forced, whether you are the one starting them or not. Wearing something that stands out makes it easier for other people to casually break the ice with you. Anything you can do to help reduce awkwardness during a conversation is a plus.

*TIP #75: Do not start a conversation with a stranger in an awkward way.

The importance of being casual when talking to strangers cannot be emphasized enough. It is really just a matter of eliminating as much awkwardness as possible.

DO: Make sure to avoid awkward ways of starting conversations with people you do not know.

DON'T: Start conversations with strangers with too much energy, formality, or tension.

The goal when you are starting a conversation with someone you do not know is to not make it a big deal in any way.

Being casual in your approach helps you put people at ease, but it also helps you get in a good mindset. If you do not think what you are doing is a big deal, you will not worry so much about being rejected or ignored. You are just throwing a comment out there and seeing whether the person wants to keep talking. If they do not want to start a conversation with you, that is perfectly fine. Just try to not be dramatic when you are starting conversations. That should be avoided at all costs.

Some examples of awkward ways to start a conversation with a stranger (things to NOT do):

1.) Walking up to someone and introducing yourself. This strategy seems innocent enough, but there is something about just walking up to someone and saying your name that makes things a little too formal, which creates awkwardness. The only exception to this advice would be if you are somewhere that is already formal, like a business event, wedding, or somewhere similar where it would be appropriate and expected. This is not usually the case in most situations, though.
2.) Starting with an apologetic comment. An apologetic comment is something like "I am sorry to bother you, but . . . " or "Forgive me for saying this, but . . . ." These kinds of phrases are counterproductive because they immediately alert the person that your upcoming comments are a big deal, as if there is some reason that you should be apologizing. If you follow my advice and start your conversations casually, there is no reason to feel like you are intruding when you do it. You may think you are being extra polite by starting a conversation by apologizing, but all you are really doing is making the conversation awkward.

There is no perfect formula for starting conversations with strangers. If you follow the advice in this tip, though, you can usually do it smoothly and gracefully.

*TIP #76: Don't be afraid of looking like you are hitting on strangers if you talk to them.

Some people are afraid to talk to strangers who are members of the opposite sex because of the possibility they might look like they are hitting on them. It is good to be careful not to be offensive, but you don't have to let this concern completely stop you from talking to them.

DO: Be sure you are respectful and casual when you talk to strangers.

DON'T: Let the fear of accidentally appearing disrespectful stop you.

As long as your intentions are good and you *aren't* actually trying to hit on people, it is definitely possible to talk to strangers without being offensive in any way. Being aware of the possibility is the first step to being able to avoid it.

There is nothing dishonorable about talking to strangers who are members of the opposite sex if you are careful to do it with class. If you follow my previous tips about starting conversations, you should be able to avoid looking creepy or pushy. If you do happen to say something that is taken badly, just try to *quickly* explain that you did not mean anything by it. Keep your comments casual and respectful when you are talking to strangers and you can feel good about yourself no matter how they are perceived.

Talking to strangers can be great for making both personal and professional connections. You should not let the outside chance that people will misunderstand your intentions stop you from trying it.

Be careful: No matter how casual and respectful you are, there is still a possibility that people could take offense if you try to talk to them. If this happens, just handle it like you would any other misunderstanding—by keeping calm and explaining yourself. You can't go through life worrying about accidentally insulting people over things you do not even mean. Keep your motives respectable and you will not have to be afraid.

Story time: This tip was inspired during a discussion I had with a potential coaching client about the benefits of talking to strangers to try to find leads for his business. This guy worked in a high-end industry where every client he got meant substantial commissions for him. He agreed that talking to strangers could make him a lot of money, but he could not get over the fear of looking like he was hitting on women. I was surprised to hear him say this and I tried to talk him into some coaching on this topic, but he would not budge. I am not trying to pressure you into doing anything that would make them uncomfortable; just realize that there are ways to talk to people you do not know in nonthreatening ways.

Chapter 4

MIDDLE OF CONVERSATIONS

*TIP #77: Be totally focused on the person you are talking to.

Most people could dramatically change the way they are perceived during conversations if they just started giving people their full attention.

DO: Give 100 percent attention to whomever you are talking to.

DON'T: Look around the room at other people as if you wish you were talking to someone else or regularly check your phone during conversations.

Whenever you are having a conversation, whether it is in a personal or professional situation, make it your goal to be completely engaged. That means you are not looking around the room, checking your phone, or only focusing on what you are going to say next. This will not only show people respect, but it will also help you process what people are saying better. It should be like they are the only thing in the world that exists.

People want to know you care about them and have an interest in what they are talking about. If you are constantly looking around the room, you are communicating that you really are not into what they are discussing. If that is true and you don't really want to talk to them, then get out of the conversation. As long as you are talking, though, do not let your attention wander. You will be much more likable that way.

*TIP #78: Do not act like you are giving a job interview when you talk to people you just met.

When you first meet someone, there may be a temptation to just ask question after question. We have all heard that one of the traits of a good conversationalist is to show interest in the other person. This is true, *but* we also should not go overboard with too many questions.

DO: Mix in questions and statements during conversations.

DON'T: Ask 100 percent questions.

There is an art to being good at talking to people. Sometimes there are obvious things to do or not do during conversations, and sometimes there are more subtle strategies to follow. Not asking too many questions almost seems backward, but it is something you should avoid.

There is no denying that most people love talking about themselves. If you spend an entire conversation with someone just asking them question after question, though, you will probably make them feel like they are in a job interview. Yuck! Nobody wants to have conversations like that. Eventually, it will just get annoying and boring. Good conversations are a combination of questions, statements, storytelling, and so on.

Be careful: I'm not saying you should keep track and literally make sure you include an equal amount of questions, comments, and stories in every conversation. Just use your common sense and use a good mix of variety to fit the situation.

*TIP #79: Tell stories during conversations.

Spice up your conversations with interesting stories.

DO: Work a story or two into your conversations if possible.

DON'T: Force stories into the conversation when they do not fit.

As was mentioned in tip #78, the best conversationalists ask questions, make statements, and tell stories. The first two are somewhat easy to do, but telling stories can be a challenge.

I am not saying you have to talk about thirty-minute epic adventures that you have had every time you talk to someone. If you can quickly work in a few interesting things that have happened to you, though, you can really help your conversational abilities.

Be careful: Be sure you use your common sense when you follow this advice. You obviously should not just tell story after story. After doing that for a while you would just become a performer and not a normal person having a normal conversation. Look for opportunities to make your conversations more interesting with a good story ONLY when it is appropriate, and you will be much more interesting.

*TIP #80: Look for something in common to talk about with people you just met.

You should not overthink the topics you discuss when you first meet someone.

DO: Try to find out if there is something you might have in common when you are talking to new people.

DON'T: Fake it and pretend like you have something in common when you really do not.

Making small talk with a stranger can be a challenge. Sometimes it might feel like there is absolutely nothing to talk about. If you can find a shared interest or experience, though, you can often make a fast connection. Maybe you have visited some of the same places, or attended the same college, or share a hobby. It doesn't really matter what common issue you share. Just try to find *something and you can probably get the conversation moving.*

Be careful: I should not even have to say this, but do not buy into this advice so much that you are willing to lie to people. If someone says that they love golf, for instance, do not pretend like you do too just to make it look like you have a shared interest. Yes, finding something in common can be a great way to connect, but if you are caught lying about it, there is a good chance you will kill any chance you had of connecting with that person.

*TIP #81: Don't be weird about eye contact.

A lot of people seem to be worried about how much eye contact they should give during conversations. How much is too much? How little is too little?

DO: Be aware of the amount of eye contact you give people, but do not obsess over it.

DON'T: Go to extremes. Try to avoid giving 100 percent or 0 percent eye contact during conversations.

Eye contact is a popular topic when it comes to the study of social skills. I have seen some experts get very specific about it, as if there is a certain magical amount that is just right. A common suggestion is to look people in the eye 100 percent of the time when we are talking to them, and others suggest 50 percent or something else. This kind of strategy is overthinking the situation. As long as you avoid the extremes and don't give *zero or total* eye contact during conversations, you will avoid looking strange.

Be careful: If you think too hard about this, you are going to be in danger of getting so obsessed about eye contact that it will be impossible to look natural no matter how much eye contact you give. So, follow my advice about not going to the extremes and you will be able to be at ease.

*TIP #82: Be aware of other people's comfort level during conversations.

Conversations are a two-way street. So don't make them all about you.

DO: Pay attention to other people's body language, reactions, and so on, to see how comfortable they are with you and what you are talking about.

DON'T: Plow through and keep talking to people without caring about how they are reacting.

A lot of people make the mistake during conversations of focusing entirely on themselves. They obsess about what they can do to look good, be comfortable, or reduce anxiety for themselves. They never think about how the other person is feeling and reacting. This is selfish thinking.

You may not have thought about it this way, but there has to be a reason for a person to keep talking to you. If all you do is talk about yourself and topics you like, they will probably lose interest quickly. It is a mistake to assume everyone is interested in the same things you are without watching how they respond.

I am not saying you have to do an intense study of people's body language to try to read their minds. Just be aware of obvious clues. If you notice someone is into what you are talking about, then, by all means, keep going. If it is clear that they are not interested, though, it is time to shorten your conversation or maybe even end it.

*TIP #83: Don't interrupt people during conversations unless you have a really good reason.

This tip is really just Social Skills 101. Unfortunately, it is broken so often that it still needs to be mentioned.

DO: Train yourself to not interrupt during conversation unless you have a *really* good reason for doing so.

DON'T: Think your comments are always more important than what the other person is talking about.

Interrupting people is just plain rude. It shows that you think what you have to say is more important than what the other person is talking about.

It is understandable why people interrupt. Sometimes when we think of something, we immediately want to say it and we just kind of blurt it out without thinking about the etiquette involved. Even if we did not really mean to do it, interrupting people still comes across as arrogant and rude, so it's best to avoid interruptions if at all possible.

I included the part about not interrupting *unless you have a really good reason* just to give you an out for special situations. If you think you absolutely *must* interrupt someone in a certain situation, in some cases that would be responsible. Sometimes there is a legitimate reason for stopping someone to make a point of your own or do something dramatic like warning them about something. Other than those extreme situations, though, interrupting people should not be a regular habit.

*TIP #84: Do not ignore the group when you approach a stranger who is already talking to other people.

Talking to strangers successfully is all about making the situation as comfortable as possible. That includes not focusing on just one person when you break into a group.

DO: Talk to groups of people you do not know.

DON'T: Immediately zero in on one person in a group and exclude everyone else.

Approaching a group of strangers can feel like a risky thing to do. There is a possibility that you might be ignored or insulted, and there is just a general risk that it could be awkward in some way. Despite the gamble, though, it is still worth trying to talk to large groups of people just because of the possibility that you might make a great connection.

Even if you do manage to get a good conversation going with one person in a group, there is still a chance that the other people there might be offended and try to stop you from talking to them. Sometimes this may be done just to pay you back for insulting the rest of the people in the group. This is why it is wise to talk to the other people there as well for a minute or two so you can make a good impression. Show respect to everyone in the group before having a one-on-one conversation with somebody, and you will have a better chance of being welcomed.

ENDING CONVERSATIONS

*TIP #85: Don't wait for the other person to end your conversation if you are ready to stop talking.

You should never feel like you are being held hostage in a conversation that you do not want to be in. It is okay to take the initiative and end it.

DO: End conversations with people you do not want to talk to anymore.

DON'T: Feel like you are at the mercy of other people's decisions to end conversations.

If you are in a business or personal social situation and you find yourself talking to someone who you do not care to talk to, there is nothing wrong with ending the conversation. If you are afraid of looking rude by doing so, there is some advice about strategically and smoothly doing so in the next tip.

*TIP #86: Use transitions to end conversations smoothly.

Once you learn how to master a few strategies for starting and continuing conversations, you will need to know about the next important step in the process—how to end them well.

DO: Use transition statements to end conversations.

DON'T: End conversations abruptly or awkwardly if it can be avoided.

There may be situations in both your personal and professional lives where you want to get out of conversations quickly. You might get caught in the middle of talking to someone at a social or work event and wish you could say goodbye without being rude. There are definitely better ways to go about this than others.

The last thing you want to do is have to figure this out in the middle of a conversation. It is hard to think on the fly without being awkward about it. That is why you should be prepared with some conversation ending transitional words and phrases just in case.

Remember, one of the fundamentals of good conversations is making them comfortable and natural. Ending them is no exception. I think the best way to do this is to use a transition comment that naturally leads to a conclusion. For instance, you might say something like "Nice meeting you," "Nice talking to you," or something similar that signals that the conversation is over. These kinds of comments make it clear that the conversation has ended without having to be awkward and say something like "I have to go now and do _____."

One exception to this strategy can occur if you talk to someone who does not recognize when you are trying to end the conversation, no matter what clues you give. When this happens, you may unfortunately have no choice but to give up on trying to be smooth about it and end things abruptly. Put off the harsh exit for as long as possible, though. It may take some planning to make your ending smooth, but it will seem completely natural if you do it well.

*TIP #87: Don't make up fake reasons to leave conversations.

There is nothing wrong with wanting to avoid awkwardness when ending conversations with strangers; just be sure you do it with integrity.

DO: Tell people why you are leaving a conversation if you think it will help make the exit smoother.

DON'T: Lie about why you are leaving a conversation just to make it less awkward.

If you want to leave a conversation, use some of the strategies mentioned in the last tip to do it smoothly. You should not feel like you owe people an explanation about why you are leaving. This is one of the reasons people sometimes think they have to lie in the first place because they feel pressure to give a great reason for wanting to move on. You don't have to give in to this pressure, though. Even if you aren't able to end the conversation smoothly, it is better to end things awkwardly than dishonestly.

Chapter 5

On the Phone (Calling, Texting, Etc.)

Communication skills apply to phone calls too. Sometimes the best strategies are the same in both situations and sometimes not.

*TIP #88: Text like you talk.

You should act like the same person no matter what method of communication you use (face-to-face, on the phone, by text, etc.)

DO: Communicate digitally the same way you would talk in person.

DON'T: Go way beyond the usual amount of pep, politeness, or positivity on the phone than you would have in person.

Authenticity should be goal number one in any situation. So, it should be obvious that the method of communication should not distract you from that.

This is not complicated. If you are a super-positive kind of person when you are face-to-face, then you should also strive to be that way digitally. If you are usually a serious person, then your texting, calling, and emailing should be similar. You should not suddenly be bubbly and peppy in digital forms of communicating just because you think people want you to be that way, or vice versa. People can spot insincerity quickly, so you are not doing yourself any favors by acting differently for different types of communication.

*TIP #89: Have good phone manners.

Have the same standards for manners on the phone that you would in person.

DO: Try to be aware of how you come across to others on the phone.

DON'T: Think that manners are not important when interacting with people you do not know well.

Little things like saying a clear hello and goodbye, not mumbling, being friendly, and so on are important when you are talking on the phone, no matter whom you are talking to. At the very least, doing these things will keep you from sounding like a dud. Even if there is a good chance that you will never speak to the person again, being friendly and treating people with respect is an admirable habit to be in.

It is amazing how many people on the phone (especially in business situations) act like they are half asleep, talking with rocks in their mouth, or are just plain rude. Even if you just tried to be aware of having good phone manners, you would already be ahead of many people.

Be careful: Do not give in to the temptation to be loose with your manners just because you can't see the person you are talking to face-to-face. You never know when you might interact with that person again.

*TIP #90: Act like you are glad to talk to people on the phone.

Talking on the phone can be intimidating, especially if you rarely do it. The best way to overcome this fear is to take charge of the main thing you can control—your attitude.

DO: Imagine that the people you talk to on the phone are already your friends.

DON'T: Be intimidated by talking to anyone on the phone.

There is similar advice about other situations in this book, but imagining that you are already friends is a strategy that works in many settings. Whether you are talking to someone in a personal situation or a professional one, there are not many times when being positive won't help you.

If you are obsessively worried that people will not like you when you call them, you are at their mercy. Your entire peace of mind depends on how they react. No, thank you! This is why the recommendation is to give yourself power over the situation and focus on having a positive mindset no matter what people do. If they do turn out to be rude or dismissive, there is often not much you could have done about it anyway. So why worry about it happening?

The good thing about having a positive attitude on the phone is that it not only makes you sound better but can also help calm your nerves. When you realize that you are in control of your attitude, it is much easier to be relaxed. Instead of filling your mind with all the bad things that might potentially happen, you are free to focus on what you are saying and hearing during the conversation. This is a powerful strategy.

Getting comfortable talking on the phone may take a little self-coaching to get your mind right at first, but it can be done. When you take control of your mindset, there is not much that can throw you off track. Even if they can't see you, your positive (or negative) attitude will show.

*TIP #91: Don't send a million text messages to someone without being answered.

An earlier tip focused on the importance of not looking needy, and phone communication is no different. When you text, call, email, or message someone, be sure you give them a reasonable amount of time to answer before you send message after message without a response.

DO: Follow up if you have not been answered after a while.

DON'T: Bother someone who has not answered quickly with more messages.

Everyone likes to be answered immediately, whether you send a casual message to a friend or a serious document to a business communication. You should not freak out, though, if you are not getting a return message immediately. If people do not answer you as quickly as you would like, do not be tempted to try to push them to hurry. If you never give people a reasonable amount of time to answer you, you will come across as pushy and desperate. These are obviously not likable traits.

Desperation and neediness not only are annoying qualities but also show a lack of self-esteem. Unless you are messaging about an emergency or something time-sensitive, do yourself a favor and chill out and let the person answer at their convenience. Don't. Be. A. Pest.

*TIP #92: Proofread texts (and other written messages) before you send them.

Your time is obviously valuable, but it is well worth taking a few extra seconds to proofread written messages before sending them.

DO: Take a quick look at your words and recipients before sending messages digitally.

DON'T: Be in such a hurry that you send the first draft of messages without looking at them.

Sending messages without reviewing what you wrote or to whom you are sending them is a risky thing to do. It could be very embarrassing if you make a mistake! You may have misspelled something, had words autocorrected into totally different words, or used bad grammar. Or worse, you may accidentally send a personal or intimate message to the wrong person.

Unfortunately, some people will be quick to judge you based on mistakes you make in messages you send to them. They are not likely to think less of you for minor mistakes, but big ones could definitely affect their opinion of you. If your grammar is bad, your intelligence could be questioned. That is not a reputation you want to have with anyone in your life, personal or professional. Be wise. Take a little extra time and be sure you are saying what you mean to say to the right person.

Story time: I have seen this mistake made in two different ways. One happens when you rush your message without proofreading it, and it gets sent with misspellings or gibberish-like words. This is not that big of a deal if you know the person receiving the text, but it can make you look dumb if it is sent to a stranger or business associate. The other way can be even more embarrassing. That happens when you do not double check on the recipient of your message. If your message contained sensitive work information or was meant for your significant other (which I have received before), this mistake could have serious consequences!

Chapter 6

Social Media Wisdom

Communication skills apply not only to face-to-face interactions but to digital and written ones as well. I realize there was no social media (or internet, for that matter) when I was eighteen years old, but I am going to give this advice as if I were that age today.

*TIP #93: Avoid saying anything digitally that you would not want to be made public.

Some people seem to think there are things we do online that are private. Not so fast! These days *anything* that is typed, spoken, or videoed onto a digital device has the potential to be made public. This is true even if you are not intentionally publishing it.

DO: Be careful what you say digitally (phone, computer, app, etc.).

DON'T: Say *anything* online you would not want to be made public.

It may seem like your phone is private, but *anything* that is recorded digitally can be shared. Texts, emails, dating app convos, and everything else you do through the internet are all recorded somewhere. That means they have the potential to be shared. So be wise, and do not do anything you would be embarrassed by if it came out later. You should almost *expect* this to happen at some point.

*TIP #94: Do not complain about your friends or your significant other on social media.

Using your social media accounts to gripe about your relationships will usually make you look worse than any behavior you are complaining about.

DO: Either tell people directly if you have a problem with them or keep it to yourself (both in person and online).

DON'T: Share your problems publicly online.

According to dictionary.com, passive-aggressive behavior is defined as "a way to express feelings of anger or annoyance, but in a non-forthcoming way." It does not get more passive-aggressive than making general or specific complaints about people on social media.

It always makes me cringe when I see people talking about their relationship problems online, whether it is a romantic one or a friendship. It is even worse if it's a general comment like "don't you hate it when men leave the toilet seat up?" as though it is meant to look like it could apply to anyone. Like people don't know that you are talking specifically about *your* person! Ugh.

If you do not like the way your significant other is acting, have some guts and handle it privately with them. Do not be childish and comment about it online for the world to see. For the sake of the relationship (and potential future ones), either talk to them directly about your issue or keep it to yourself instead. You may not only damage the trust you have with that person but could also make yourself look bad to the people who are connected with you.

*TIP #95: Do not share too much of your personal business on social media.

Transparency is "in" these days. But there are some things that should just not be shared publicly.

DO: Have a legitimate purpose for sharing private information about your life.

DON'T: Use social media as your personal therapy session.

There are times when sharing personal things online can be useful. It can help your business if potential clients notice you. Friends can learn something about you that they do not already know. But do not make the mistake of thinking that sharing *everything* about yourself is a good idea.

There is definitely a line you can cross where you can share too much. For instance, complaining about every little annoyance you have on social media is probably not a great look. You should also be careful not to share too much information (TMI) about personal things. All these things will do is annoy your connections, and yet some people still seem to think doing this is a good idea!

There are simply some things about you that everyone does not need to know. If you absolutely must make your life an open book, at least do it because you want to and not because you feel pressured. There is no reason to feel *obligated* to share everything about yourself in the name of transparency. And let's be honest, it is a little creepy to share certain things about our lives. Even if these are not good enough reasons to keep your life private, do you really want to force your problems on people who have not given you permission to do so?

*TIP #96: Don't "like," retweet, comment, or share things on other people's social media at 3 a.m.

There are some people who will read deep meaning into your activity on social media, including the times you respond.

DO: Be aware of the time of day you answer people's social media posts.

DON'T: "Like," retweet, comment, or share things on other people's social media late at night.

This may seem like a random issue to bring up, but there are some common social media "mistakes" that may not always be obvious. Some people may make assumptions about your intent without really knowing the truth, but you can still be judged poorly if you do these things.

Be careful: It is a good idea to take the unofficial rules of social media communication seriously. For instance, responding to somebody's social media posts at 3 a.m. may give the impression that you are thinking of the person in the middle of the night. Uh oh! It does not matter if you were really flirting or just happened to be up at that time. Your actions could be interpreted differently and cause problems.

I know you probably would not intend to express some deep meaning if you did these kinds of things, but it is best to play it safe. Even if you did want to express interest in someone, late-night comments would not be the smoothest way to go about it. You are better off just staying off of social media late at night, whether there is a secret meaning behind your comments or not.

*TIP #97: Try to answer every single person who comments on your social media posts.

Unless you become famous and get a million followers, do not get so distracted that you forget to answer people who respond to you in a friendly way on social media.

DO: Respond any time someone makes a friendly comment to you online.

DON'T: Ignore people who comment on you.

It takes time and effort for someone to write something on your social media page. Even if you are just "liking" what they say, you should still make it your goal to answer every single friendly comment made to you online. This is true whether they are your best friend or a complete stranger. And do not make the excuse that you have no time to do it. You should be so flattered that someone made the effort to reach out to you at all that you *make* time to show that person gratitude with an answer.

This advice does not apply if someone says something negative or creepy to you, of course. This is not to suggest that you thank people for insulting you. That would be silly. It also does not mean that you answer negative people with your own negative comment to get back at them. The point of this advice is to show appreciation when it is deserved.

In those cases where someone does say something negative to you online, you should probably have the *opposite* reaction and say nothing at all. Unless you want to get involved in a debate or argument, do not feel like you have to save your reputation just because some random person insulted you. It's just not worth the trouble it can cause. If you absolutely feel like you must respond, make a very casual, dismissive, or even humorous comment. Online fights do nothing but make you look bad. You are better off avoiding them.

Story time: I am not famous by any means, but I do write frequently on social media. Even if a post of mine gets a lot of attention, though, I always try to answer every comment to me. I feel obligated to show my appreciation for the effort that was made.

Chapter 7

General Communication and Social Skills at Work

Communication and social skills are just as important in professional situations as they are in our personal lives. They can help or hurt your chances for success, happiness, and job security.

*TIP #98: Respect authority unless given a reason not to.

Having respect for authority is not only the right thing to do; it is the smart thing to do.

DO: Respect your bosses, teachers, parents, coaches, and anyone else in an authoritative position over you.

DON'T: Follow orders that make you compromise your morals.

When someone is in a position of authority over you, they are in that role for a reason. Maybe they are a parent, boss, or someone in another kind of leadership role. It makes sense that you have a general respect for them unless they do something to lose it.

People seem to respect authority a lot less these days than they used to. We are living more and more in a culture of suspicion. It seems like we have gone from automatically respecting authority to *disrespecting authority* at first unless they prove themselves to be worthy. That is backward thinking. Be different from most people and show respect from the beginning.

Be careful: I am not suggesting blind allegiance to authority figures who abuse their power or show a lack of character. If someone asks you to do something that you know is unethical or against your morals, there is nothing wrong with refusing to comply. Just make sure that you have a really good reason if you are going to take a stand like that because it could get you fired, disliked, and so on. And before you decide to stand up to every authority figure in your life, realize that disrespecting people who are in charge just because you do not want to do what they ask you to do is not a legitimate reason to challenge them.

*TIP #99: Do not publicly insult your coworkers.

Let's face it, sometimes our coworkers can be jerks. Most people are friendly, but it is inevitable that some will be hard to get along with. That is just life. It does not mean you have a right to share your negative opinions about them publicly.

DO: Make your best effort to get along with your coworkers.

DON'T: Criticize them to others.

If you have a problem with someone you work with, the best thing to do is to handle it there in private. What you should *not* do is say negative things about them in public, including social media posts. No good will come from doing that.

If you make a habit of publicly insulting or gossiping about coworkers, whether it is in person or online, you can bet that it will get back to them. And it should not be a surprise if they hate you for it. Maybe you will not care if that happens, but it is still not a great situation to have people think that way about you. Another result may be that you will look bad to the people you are talking *to* as well. You lose either way.

Be careful: Before you try to argue with this point by saying gossip is okay as long as it is based on truth, realize that it can still make you look bad even when it is true. Yes, spreading lies about people is nasty behavior, but even spreading negative TRUTHS about people can make them mad sometimes.

*TIP #100: Don't complain publicly about your boss.

If you should not insult your coworkers in public (as mentioned in tip #99), then you should definitely not openly criticize your boss. That is just asking for trouble.

DO: Give constructive criticism privately to your boss if you think it could help.

DON'T: Criticize your boss to your coworkers.

Complaining seems to be a hobby for some people. They complain about everything they do not like about their lives, jobs, family, friends, and so on. Some do it online and others do it in person. Other than the fact that it makes you look like a whiner, it can also do serious damage to your job security if you complain about your boss or supervisor. Doing this may get on their bad side or it may even be a fireable offense.

Be careful: It seems like every workplace has an employee who loves telling on their coworkers so they can score points with the boss. Realize that anything you say has a chance to get back to the top. Be wise and use some common sense about whom you complain to and what you complain about.

*TIP #101: Return work emails, calls, and texts ASAP.

An earlier tip mentioned the importance of speedy responses for general situations. But it applies even more when you are communicating about work-related issues.

DO: Answer work-related emails, calls, text, and so on as soon as possible during business hours.

DON'T: Delay answering unless you are contacted outside of business hours.

Sometimes in business, the goal is to help separate yourself from the competition. Little things like answering quickly can help you do that. On the other hand, responding too slowly can cause you to lose business to someone who is more attentive. When that is a possibility, you know it is an issue to take seriously.

Be careful: The reason I included the exception of not feeling obligated to answer outside of business hours is because you probably do not want to set an expectation for being on call 24/7. You should not be so obsessed with answering quickly that you feel like you never have a break from work. That is a good way to drive yourself crazy.

Just use your common sense. If you have a job that involves deadlines that need immediate attention, then you may need to be available during random times. In general, though, do whatever you can to answer ASAP when someone gets in touch with you during reasonable hours.

Story time: I have always tried to answer people's messages in a reasonable amount of time, but I never fully appreciated the importance of it until I worked as a real estate agent. In industries like these that are dependent on building relationships, your answer speed habits can make the difference between success and failure. Answering too slowly could even be the reason that someone chooses your competition over you.

*TIP #102: Follow the karma business strategy.

Karma is a word that can have many different meanings, but the connection here relates to business. In a general sense, karma means that good things will happen to you in the long run if you do good, and bad things will happen to you if you do bad. This principle definitely applies to career-related relationships.

DO: Be good to people whenever you can.

DON'T: Expect to be rewarded by everyone you are good to.

I am a big believer in the business karma strategy (do good and good will back to you), but it does not necessarily work on a case-by-case basis. It is possible that you might help someone in some way and never hear from that person again. Or even worse, they may even be mean to you despite your kindness. If you are thinking big picture, though, negative reactions to your good behavior will not matter much because you will most likely be rewarded more often than not. The overall result will still be positive.

The point of this strategy is not to create some kind of good deed balance sheet that will eventually pay off for you. The goal of business karma is to make a positive impact on people and hopefully get rewarded *over time*. If your goal is to make every person you help immediately return the favor, then you are really just attempting to make a transaction with them. That is not what this is about.

The business karma strategy is more of a long-term numbers game than a short-term return-on-investment goal. The idea is that if you help enough people, you will be rewarded by a certain percentage of them over time. There is probably no official case study to prove that this works, but it makes sense that it works.

This way of thinking may sound selfish, as if you are only being good to people so they will help you later. This is the case, though. While getting rewarded is one of the benefits of using this approach, it is just one of the reasons for doing it. For one thing, being good to people as a way of life is just more fun! Helping someone get a job, get business, make connections, and so on makes you feel good even if you get no other return out of it. Plus, it is just the right thing to do.

*TIP #103: Be careful about talking about sensitive subjects like politics, religion, and even sports at work.

Unfortunately, some people just do not handle it well when someone disagrees with them—about anything. No matter how carefully and politely you phrase your comments about some topics, you could still make people angry if your opinion does not match theirs.

DO: Be careful about the topics you discuss socially at work.

DON'T: Assume people will not mind if you think differently than they do.

It is possible that you will see some of your coworkers day after day for many years. That means that if you make enemies, you will be stuck with them for a long time! It makes sense then that you should be careful about the battles you start with people at work. If they disagree with you about something, sometimes it is best just to let it go. Even if you think you can prove that you are right, it will be a hollow victory if the result is a broken relationship. Sometimes it is just better to keep quiet.

Be careful: If you enjoy debating and discussing a variety of topics and can do so without getting upset, you don't have to worry about looking bad yourself. Everybody does not think that way, though. Some people just can't handle a simple disagreement, and they can get ugly about it fast. It is unfortunate to have to deal with conflict like this at work, especially for something that could have been avoided.

*TIP #104: Do not tell inappropriate jokes at work.

Having a sense of humor can make your work environment more enjoyable for both you and your coworkers. There can be a fine line between being funny and being offensive, however.

DO: Show your humorous side at work.

DON'T: Tell jokes that have hidden (or not so hidden) sexual innuendos.

It is not a good idea to risk getting yourself in trouble just for trying to be funny. We spend a lot of time with our coworkers, sometimes more than with our own families. It can be tempting to joke with people at work as we get comfortable with them, but you can't give in to the temptation to do this. When we are in a professional environment, there have to be stricter boundaries on the way we use humor.

Be careful: The obvious jokes you should avoid are the kinds that are sexual in any way. You should also stay away from anything that makes fun of certain groups of people. You could be reprimanded or even fired for it! It is just not worth the risk just to try to get a laugh.

*TIP #105: Always follow through with your promises at work (big and small).

If you are not true to your word, you simply can't be trusted. That is not a reputation you want to have at work.

DO: Be obsessed with keeping your word at work.

DON'T: Keep your promises only when you think it is important.

There are not many things worse to be known for than being untrustworthy, especially in a work environment. You should make it your goal to *always, always, always* do what you say you are going to do for your coworkers, clients, employer, and so on. When you show that you can be dependable for things that are not that big of a deal, bigger opportunities will probably come your way.

Be careful: Some people are only serious about keeping their word if it is about something urgent or important. While this is better than nothing, my recommendation is to do your best to follow through with EVERYTHING you promise to do, big or small. Do not let the situation affect how serious you are about doing what you say you will do.

*TIP #106: Go above and beyond with customer service.

Whether you are running your own business or working for someone else, customer service is an easy thing to control. Being known for treating people better than they expect will help you stand out from the competition.

DO: Deliver more to customers and clients than what is reasonable in attitude and general service.

DON'T: Do just enough to get by.

Some people may think customer service is only important if you work in sales, retail, or restaurants. That is not true. Any job where you interact with the public is affected by the way you treat people. Be sure you take this responsibility seriously.

As the saying goes, you should "under promise and over deliver." Your customers and clients usually have choices other than you, so it is essential that you are as likable and productive as possible. If you can figure out a way to surprise people with the greatness of your service, success is sure to follow.

*TIP #107: Don't believe the idea that you have to be dishonest to be successful in business.

The belief that the only way to be successful in business is to be ruthless or immoral is a myth that was probably created by movies and television. The truth is that many of the most successful businesspeople have very high character.

DO: Act with integrity in your business career.

DON'T: Cut corners to try to get ahead.

Many of the wealthiest people in the world have given away a *lot* of money to various charitable causes and volunteered their time for many worthy organizations. I realize that this does not automatically make them saints, but it should put an end to the rumor that all wealthy people are penny-pinching scrooges. The best businesses in the world are usually founded on the principles of honesty, loyalty, and treating employees and customers well. Most of them operate with class and integrity as well.

Even if you could get ahead with less-than-honorable business practices, would you even feel good about it? Most people probably wouldn't. And if that is not a concern for you, your reputation could still be ruined if you are caught doing something you shouldn't be doing. In these times of increasing transparency, you probably won't be able to get away with anything anyway.

*TIP #108: Do not break or change plans for meetings with professional contacts if at all possible.

This is a rule that should be followed obsessively. When you make plans with someone in a business situation, you should do whatever you can to keep that appointment.

DO: Keep your word about plans you make with business contacts.

DON'T: Break plans casually in business situations.

When you break plans with someone, you are disrupting their day in some way. It does not matter how good your excuse was for doing it. This is why you should not back out of scheduled appointments for frivolous reasons like having to catch up on your to-do list.

For some people, having to change plans can be very inconvenient, especially if it is done at the last minute. Your reputation depends on how you handle these situations. Also, if you break enough appointments with some people, eventually they will stop making plans with you at all.

This advice is especially important if you have agreed to meet people you do not know. You are risking losing touch with them if you break or change plans even once. Do not do it unless something that is out of your control happens to keep you away.

*TIP #109: Smile and be friendly when you work with the public, even if you are in a bad mood.

If you ever have a job where you must work with the public, like retail, food service, and so on, you should do your best to have a positive attitude when you are interacting with them—no matter what kind of mood you are in.

DO: Make it your goal to always have great customer service.

DON'T: Show a bad mood or attitude when you are working with customers.

Some people say you should always be transparent and wear your emotions on your sleeve. While I do think we should generally strive to be authentic and real, that does not mean you always have to let your mood show publicly. This is *especially true* if you have a customer service job.

If you have a job where you are in view of customers, it does not matter if you had a fight with your spouse before you came to work, got some bad news, or had some other bad thing happen to you. You must show positivity. If you do not think you can handle that, then you should probably not get a job where customer service matters.

The only exception to this rule would be if something so bad happened that you can't even reasonably pretend to be okay, like a death in the family or something like that. It would be unreasonable to suggest that that you should act like there's nothing wrong. If something that serious happens, though, you probably should not be coming in to work anyway.

Staying positive is a crucial part of customer service and professional likability. If you are in a management position, you should push to make it a priority for your employees. Everybody talks about it, but not every company is committed to it.

Story time: When I coached high school basketball, I had a rule for my players that I did not want the spectators to be able to tell if we were winning or losing based on our body language and effort. The same thing is true for customer service. Don't let customers be able to tell if you are in a bad mood based on your behavior in front of them. Fake it if you have to.

*TIP #110: Don't complain about your problems (personal or professional) when you are around customers.

Complaining in front of customers is bad for business, no matter what it is about.

DO: Keep your problems to yourself when your customers or clients can hear you.

DON'T: Ever complain *to* customers.

It's understandable that people will sometimes have had a bad day at work, but if you have a customer service job you still can't show it. Yes, you have a right to feel that way. What you do *not* have a right to do is talk about those things in front of customers. You shouldn't complain directly *to* your customers or even within earshot of them. It's just not professional and it will make the company that you are working for look bad.

Feel free to complain to your friends or significant other at home if you want to, or maybe even complain to your coworkers behind the scenes. Just never ever do it in front of your customers. They want a great experience at your place of business, not negative energy.

*TIP #111: Do not wear sunglasses when you meet with people you don't know well.

Wearing sunglasses may make you feel cool, but wearing them during a business meeting could make you look unprofessional, even if it is outside. It is worse if you do not know the people well who you are meeting.

DO: Feel free to wear sunglasses when talking to someone you know well.

DON'T: Wear sunglasses when you are meeting with people you do not know well.

Our eyes communicate a lot about what we are thinking. They can show approval or disapproval, kindness or hostility, and much more. Don't cover them up when you are talking to someone in a professional situation and hide one of the main ways you communicate with people.

*TIP #112: Always have great phone manners at work.

If you have to talk to customers or clients on the phone as part of your job, make sure you act like a professional.

DO: Talk to people during work phone calls like you are glad to talk to them.

DON'T: Go overboard and get *too* peppy or casual if it is a work-related conversation.

If you ever talk to people on the phone when they are at work, you probably notice that many of them either act stuffy or cranky. There is no excuse for this kind of behavior and no reason you can't fix it easily if it applies to you. Your company depends on you to make a good impression on them.

Be careful; I said to not go overboard with your friendliness on work calls because there is a point where too much positivity can be fake and annoying. You should act like you are glad to talk to people, but not like a puppy who hasn't seen his owner all day.

*TIP #113: Don't be afraid to cold call, cold email, or cold DM.

Cold calling often has a bad reputation, whether it is done on the phone or in other ways like emailing or walk-ins. If you do it well, though, cold calling can be a great way to find leads and make connections with people.

DO: Use cold calling, cold email, cold DM, and so on if you think it could help your business.

DON'T: Shy away from cold calling just because you think it will make you look bad.

Yes, it is true that cold calling is sometimes known for being annoying, but that is usually because it has been done poorly. If you do it the right way, cold calling is a perfectly reasonable and acceptable method of business development. It starts with being respectful and friendly. You do not want to be so pushy that you make people uncomfortable.

Contacting strangers about potential business can be a successful tactic. Just be sure that you do not contribute to the already bad reputation that it has by using questionable methods.

*TIP #114: Do not be dishonest in any way at work (not even white lies).

There are not many things that can hurt your reputation as much as dishonesty.

DO: Make it your goal to say what you mean and mean what you say.

DON'T: Be casual with the truth about minor things.

Being dishonest can make you appear to be untrustworthy, even if it is about something small. You will be doing yourself a favor if you establish a reputation for telling the truth in any situation.

Not being casual with the truth about "minor things" is included because it can be tempting to only be as honest as the circumstances call for. In other words, there is a temptation to be more honest the more serious the situation but not so much for more minor things. While it is true that some lies are bigger than others, it is still a good idea to try to avoid telling them at all.

Even if you do not have a problem with the immorality part of lying, you never know when you might get caught doing it. When that happens, even if it is for something small, your reputation can be damaged severely and permanently. It is just not a gamble worth taking.

*TIP #115: Don't drink too much coffee, soda, or alcohol before professional events.

This seems like it should probably be common sense, but it is always best to have total control of yourself when you are in work-related social situations. That means being careful not to drink too much alcohol, and you might even want to limit the amount of caffeine you have as well.

DO: Limit yourself to one drink of coffee, soda, or alcohol before professional events.

DON'T: Drink alcohol just because it is free.

Be careful: Even one drink of coffee, soda, or alcohol can throw you off your game. It would be a shame to lose out on a possible great connection because you were too hyper from drinking too much caffeine or too tipsy from drinking alcohol. I realize everyone is affected differently by these things and you may still be okay after a drink or two. But maybe not. It is not worth the risk.

*TIP #116: Use good grammar in professional situations.

Whether you are talking or writing, you should always be careful to use good grammar when you are communicating with someone in a career setting.

DO: Be careful to use good grammar, especially if you are speaking or writing something publicly.

DON'T: Be so afraid of making one grammar mistake that you stress yourself out over it.

It is not the worst thing in the world if you make a grammar mistake. We all mess up every now and then, and most people are not experts at every grammar rule that exists. Some people associate grammar skills with intelligence, though, so it is possible that you could be judged if your mistakes are too dramatically bad or too frequent.

Be careful: You should not be so worried about making grammar mistakes that you get uptight and stressed out about it. An occasional slip-up is not going to be a big deal. Just be careful about what you say and double-check what you write so you can avoid obvious mistakes.

Chapter 8

Leadership

Communication skills are an essential part of successful leadership.

*TIP #117: Overcommunicate your expectations when you are in a leadership position.

Communication is everything in leadership. To be a successful leader, you must be clear about your goals, expectations, potential consequences, and more. Even if it means that you are risking being a little annoying, it is essential that you communicate well with the people you are leading.

DO: Communicate clearly when you are in a leadership position.

DON'T: Assume people understand you.

A common cause of frustration for leaders occurs when people do not meet expectations. If you are a leader and this is a problem you face, be sure to look at yourself first before assigning blame. Did you explain the expectations that were not met well enough? Were you clear about what would happen if people did not meet those expectations? Do not be the type of leader who gets upset at mistakes that were caused by a lack of clear direction by YOU.

*TIP #118: Use both praise and criticism when you are in a position of leadership.

A big part of leadership is motivation, and it is not always easy to do. You have to be able to make people feel good about themselves when they do well but also correct them when they don't meet expectations.

DO: Make an effort to praise good behavior and offer constructive criticism when necessary.

DON'T: Go too far in either direction.

Willingness to use both praise and criticism are essential skills for leaders. If you can be positive when things are going well and critical when people mess up, you will prove that your words can be trusted. When you do that, you show that your goal is to speak the truth, not manipulate. People accept criticism much easier when they know that they will also be praised when they do well.

Be careful: Either criticizing or praising too much could have terrible results. If all you do is criticize, you will be thought of as a bully. If all you do is praise, you will look like a kiss up. There must be a balance if you want to be respected as an honest and fair leader.

*TIP #119: Don't act like a know-it-all.

Be careful about how you talk about topics that you know a lot about. Bragging about your knowledge can make you lose people's respect.

DO: Be confident when you get an opportunity to talk about a topic you know well.

DON'T: Act like you are better than others when you talk about topics you are an expert in.

Most people are very knowledgeable about *something*. Maybe you are great at fishing, sports, the stock market, or something else. When you have a chance to show off your knowledge about a topic, though, be sure you are not acting arrogantly about it just because you know more than everyone else. You are not better than everyone just because you are good at that one thing. I am sure that there are plenty of things you are not good at as well. Stay humble.

There is nothing wrong with being confident in your abilities, but when it turns into arrogance you become a jerk. It is okay to use your knowledge to contribute to a conversation; just be sure you act with class when you do.

*TIP #120: Be unemotional when you discipline.

If you are in a leadership position of any kind, chances are that you will have to be a disciplinarian at some point. How you handle this part of your job can be the difference between success and failure.

DO: Let your consequences alone be the punishment when you have to discipline someone.

DON'T: Combine consequences with anger or intimidation.

The actual disciplinary methods you use are less important than the attitude you have when you implement them. The best thing you can do when handling behavior issues is to be as calm and unemotional as possible; otherwise there is a good chance that you will do more harm than good. Unreasonable anger and attitude will make you lose respect as a leader, especially if you have those reactions every time you discipline someone.

We have probably all experienced leaders who do not follow this advice. Whatever consequences they administer often come with a negative attitude of some kind—no matter how severe the mistake. The problem with this kind of leadership is that it can break people's spirit, which means your effectiveness will also suffer.

When you give consequences without anger or attitude, it is a lot easier to keep your relationships strong. Most people understand that bad behavior leads to negative consequences. What they may not accept is being disrespected in the process.

Story time: When I first started teaching high school, I was not very good with discipline. My main strategy was to react to situations in the moment. The result was that I would either be too strict or too lenient, with not much else in between. This made it difficult for my students to know what to expect from me, which is never good. As soon as I got more organized and less emotional, though, discipline became a strength. This strategy can help you whether you are a boss, parent, teacher, coach, or in any other leadership position that requires you to be a disciplinarian.

Chapter 9

Public Speaking

Communication skills include more than just one-on-one interactions. The ability to speak publicly with confidence and effectiveness in various settings can also help you find more success, peace, and happiness.

*TIP #121: Commit to being yourself when you give a presentation or speech.

It is natural to want to be liked, especially when we are speaking publicly. There is nothing wrong with wanting to be likable; just be careful not to let this goal tempt you to be fake.

DO: Be authentic when you are speaking publicly.

DON'T: Be fake to try to impress your audience.

Committing to being yourself during a speech can be tough to do. You may feel like you need to try to put on an act in some way to be credible or to win the audience over. This is a risky game to play, though, because if it backfires, you will lose them.

People can usually spot insincerity easily. You may think you are fooling your audience by trying to be someone you aren't, but you probably aren't. And when you are caught being insincere, it sends a message that you can't be trusted.

Being yourself not only makes you look better to the audience, but it also helps your peace of mind. Pretending you are someone you are not can be exhausting because you have to constantly think about keeping up your fake personality. That is a lot of pressure to put on yourself. When you are comfortable being authentic, it is much easier to relax and be at peace with yourself.

Be careful: About the only thing that might be reasonable to fake during a speech is confidence (see tip #11). If you are feeling nervous, acting like you are confident can actually make you believe that you are. Just do not try too hard or you will look worse than if you had no confidence at all. Changing your entire personality is hard to pull off, though.

If you commit to being yourself during presentations, be sure to accept the fact that some people may not like you. However, that would be true whether it is the fake you or the real you anyway! So why waste time worrying about it.

*TIP #122: Overprepare for speeches and presentations.

Unless you have a gift for thinking on your feet, the last thing you should do when you are speaking in public is try to wing it. That is why you should plan as much as possible ahead of time, even to the point of being overprepared.

DO: Figure out whatever a reasonable amount of preparation would be for your presentation and then do more.

DON'T: Stop preparing when you think you have done just enough to get by.

When you speak publicly, you have a responsibility to do as well as you can. People are giving up their valuable time to listen to you, so you should take it lightly. Being well prepared for a presentation or speech will make you look good, but it also shows respect for your audience.

Being overprepared is also a good strategy for calming your nerves. If public speaking anxiety is a problem for you, you should try to eliminate all the possible causes of nervousness that you possibly can. The stress that is caused by not being completely sure what you are going to say is one way to do this.

Be careful: I am a big believer in the effectiveness of overpreparing, but you should still try to avoid obsessing about it. There is a point where too much perfectionism in your preparation can be counterproductive. It can do more harm than good if it stresses you out.

Story time: When I was in college, a drama class I was taking required us to do a two-person scene. My partner and I planned to practice all weekend to get ready for it. Unfortunately, the day before we were going to start practicing, she called me and said her parents had called her home (in another city) for the weekend. As a result, we had zero practice time. I was extremely nervous about the scene, but it taught me a valuable lesson—if I ever have the chance to prepare before a public performance, I would do it as much as possible. I never want to be in that position of uncertainty again if I can help it.

*TIP #123: Have a hard beginning and hard ending when public speaking.

This is just a little practical advice. A good speech almost always has a clear (if not dramatic) opening and closing, whether it is a summary of the talk, an interesting story, or some other way to give the presentation a little umph at the beginning and end.

DO: Have an interesting beginning to your presentations to "hook" your audience and a clear ending.

DON'T: Make your presentations one long stream of information.

A lot of speakers almost seem to start in the middle of their presentations. In other words, they kind of just start talking and then they eventually just stop talking. There is no clear organization to what they are doing. It comes across as disorganized and boring. This may be a good format if you are giving a technical talk about something like medical facts, but it is a terrible style if your goal is to be interesting. There may be people in your audience who are a little skeptical about you at first as well, so you may have to do a few things to spark their interest.

A good starting place to hook your audience is to try to convince them that your topic is worthwhile. If that point is not established, then everything you say is a waste of time. You should explain why your content is worth listening to, why it will help them make money, entertain them, make them think, or whatever reason fits your topic. It doesn't have to be anything fancy; just be sure you have *something* prepared to inspire them to pay attention early on.

Once you have your opening taken care of, you can now smoothly move on to your main content. Then at the end you can close it nicely with a summary of what you talked about or some other clear way to end it.

You do not have to be fancy to make great presentations, but there are some little things you can do with your structure to help your cause. That begins with having a clear beginning, middle, and ending.

*TIP #124: Always try to end your presentations ON TIME.

There is something unsettling about being told that a presentation will be over in a certain amount of time and having it go longer than promised. It can feel like *torture*. So be respectful of your audience when you speak, and make it a priority to finish exactly when you said you would.

DO: Be obsessed with finishing your presentation when you say you will.

DON'T: Be casual about your stated end time and go over by even a few minutes.

Even if your presentation is enjoyable, there is just something annoying about being promised an end time and having that promise broken. People usually will not mind giving someone their attention for a reasonable amount of time, but once the ending has been established, the promise should be kept.

It almost does not make sense that this is a big deal, but it is. A forty-five-minute speech that is promised to be over in an hour will be received better than the exact same forty-five-minute speech that is promised to be over in thirty minutes. There is just something about preparing our mind for the amount of time needed to pay attention that is uncomfortable if broken.

I understand why speakers make this mistake. They think they are doing something positive for the audience by promising that they are almost finished, as if the promise itself will make the audience feel better. That may be true in the short term, but the disappointment of not having it end at the given time outweighs the positive feelings resulting from the promise. Sometimes speakers will even go *way* past the promised end time. These speakers clearly don't get it.

Whether the end time was promised in the advertising for your event or if you mention it during your presentation, be sure you stick to your promise. Do yourself a favor and even go as far as *obsessing* about sticking to the promised finishing time. Your audience will appreciate you for it.

*TIP #125: Don't admit to being nervous during a speech.

Telling your audience that you are nervous at the beginning of your speech may seem like a good way to get sympathy, but it might actually hurt your credibility.

DO: Accept nervousness during a presentation as being normal.

DON'T: Say that you are nervous.

I know that multiple tips in this book stress the importance of being real and authentic, but that does not mean you have to share everything you are thinking. It is okay to keep some things to yourself, including how nervous you are.

The audience would understand and forgive you if you look nervous, and most of them would probably be nervous too if they were in your place. Just avoid trying to make them feel sorry for you by actually saying it. Even if people do sympathize with you, that is still not enough of a reason for them to listen to your talk. It's best to act like you are a credible speaker and not bring attention to the anxiety you may be feeling (even if you are nervous).

*TIP #126: Be interesting, entertaining, or dramatic—if you can't be any of those things, be brief.

Some speakers can ramble on during a presentation and still be interesting. It is a gift that not many people have. If you do not have a talent for improv-type public speaking, be sure you make your presentations as short as possible.

DO: Make your presentation worth listening to.

DON'T: Ramble.

No matter what your presentation is about and no matter who your target audience is, you should always consider how it will look from their perspective. Whether you are presenting dry facts in a presentation at work or talking on stage as a stand-up comedian, the objective of your presentation should still be to provide value. For most people in your audience, that means making it shorter.

*TIP #127: Make eye contact with your audience.

Making eye contact when you are public speaking may not seem like that big of a deal, but people notice. They may even think less of you if you do not give enough of it.

DO: Make eye contact with random members of the audience.

DON'T: Look too far down or above the audience.

Making eye contact during presentations has benefits that you may not even realize. It engages the audience, makes you appear more friendly, and shows confidence. It is an underrated part of good public speaking skills.

If the audience is somewhat large, you obviously can't make eye contact with everyone. So how should you handle this challenge? In that case, you just have to give the *illusion* that you are looking at everyone. You can do this by moving your eyes around the room and making eye contact with a few audience members in different sections as you do. This will make it look like you are engaged with the whole group. Whatever strategy you use for making eye contact, be sure you make it a priority.

*TIP #128: Involve the audience when you are public speaking, if possible.

Get your audience thinking and talking early in your presentation, and you will have a much better chance of holding their attention.

DO: Ask your audience questions when you speak publicly (even if they are rhetorical).

DON'T: Ask too many questions of your audience.

There are two things that every audience loves to do: show off and feel included. When you ask them questions, you give your audience a chance to do both. This will not only help you connect with them, but it will also increase their engagement as your presentation goes on.

I realize there may be some settings where it is not possible to get feedback from the audience. If you are talking to a crowd of 10,000 people, this idea will obviously not work very well. When that happens, you could still ask questions that the audience can answer to themselves. Anything you do to give your audience a feeling that they are participants and not just observers is a plus.

Be careful: The types of questions you ask make a difference too. Ask things that have factual answers, not just asking for opinions that won't really let your audience show off. Give them a chance to be right and show their knowledge, and you will have them on your side from the beginning.

*TIP #129: Do not overvalue the importance of your presentations.

One cause of public speaking anxiety is thinking that your presentation is a bigger deal than it actually is. Keep things in perspective and you will have a much better chance of keeping your mind at ease.

DO: Make sure your presentation is as good as it can be.

DON'T: Think it is so important that it paralyzes you into not being able to perform well at all.

Anytime you are talking to an audience, there is a degree of importance to what you are discussing. Even if your goal is just to entertain people, it matters. The question though is how much. Obviously, the significance of your topic increases if it impacts something serious like your job or wellbeing, or the wellbeing of others. If you want to keep a positive mindset, it is important that you keep the information you are sharing in perspective. As soon as you overvalue the impact of what you are doing, you run the risk of causing unnecessary stress for yourself.

What is the worst thing that could happen if your performance does not go well? Would you be embarrassed? Would you miss out on a business opportunity? Even if the worst possible outcome would be something terrible like losing your job, it would still not be the end of the world. Don't treat every public speaking situation like it is a life-or-death situation, and you will be much more comfortable.

*TIP #130: Do not mumble when public speaking.

When you are giving a presentation, an obvious goal should be to speak clearly enough to be heard and understood.

DO: Enunciate your words and project your voice when giving a presentation.

DON'T: Speak too quickly or mumble.

Whether you are speaking for a grade, a job, or just to be entertaining, there is a reason that people are listening to you. You have a responsibility to respect their time and attention and make your presentation as clear and interesting as possible. That starts with making your words easy to hear and understand.

One way to guard against a mumbling problem when you are speaking publicly is to make sure you are as comfortable as possible. Social anxiety can make us speed up our words and not pronounce everything like we would in normal conversation. You can use some of my earlier tips in this book if you need to get your mind more at ease during presentations to help you with this. Improving your comfort level can do a lot to help you speak more confidently and clearly.

Be careful: Being able to enunciate your words will also make you come across as more intelligent, even if the words you are saying are not actually that deep. Just don't take it too far, of course. Over-enunciating can sound bad too.

Talking quickly or mumbling may just be the way you usually talk. If that is the case, you may want to video yourself speaking and see if you can catch anything that needs correcting. You could also ask someone to watch you and give you feedback about your speaking style. Do whatever it takes to learn how to speak as clearly as possible because being understood is obviously a key part of public speaking success.

*TIP #131: Do not chew gum when giving a speech.
If public speaking makes you nervous, it is important that you try to figure out ways to overcome your anxiety. Chewing gum should not be one of those strategies.
DO: Find ways to lower your anxiety during presentations.
DON'T: Chew gum to accomplish it.

I know that chewing gum may help you calm your nerves, but it is not worth the negative effect it has on your appearance when you are speaking publicly. There is just something about chewing gum that makes you look like you aren't taking your presentation seriously. It is kind of strange that this is true, but for whatever reason, chewing gum can make us look casual, aloof, or even less intelligent.

There may not even be a great reason that chewing gum has this negative association, but it does. Don't waste time and energy making the case that it shouldn't be that way. Just realize that it does and don't fight it. Leave the gum at home when you have an important presentation and find another way to relax.

*TIP #132: Don't get obsessed worrying about saying space filler words like "uh," "um," and "you know."
Using words like "uh," "um," and "you know" are classic public speaking mistakes. It is definitely not good if you say those things often, but you shouldn't be so worried about saying them that you get stressed out about it.
DO: Try your best to avoid saying filler words like "um" and "you know."
DON'T: Be so obsessed about avoiding space filler words that it makes you worry about it during your presentation.

Public speaking is difficult for a lot of reasons. It can take a lot of time to prepare for, people in your audience may not understand what you are trying to say, and it can cause severe anxiety. But there is another reason that speaking publicly is tough for a lot of people—the paranoia that has often been caused by public speaking teachers about saying the forbidden words "uh," "um," and "you know."

Yes, it is a good idea in general to try to avoid using these kinds of space filler words and phrases. Just be sure you keep this mistake in perspective. You should not get so obsessed about it that it gets in the way of your performance.

Contrary to what your public speaking teacher may have told you, it is not the end of the world if you say "um" once or twice during your talk. You should not beat yourself up if you do. If you listen to even the most famous broadcasters and public speakers, you will even hear them say those words every now and then! If they do it, I think it will be okay if you occasionally do too.

Be careful: All you really need to avoid is saying these words TOO MUCH. Other than that, I would not be concerned if an "um" or "you know" occasionally slips out when you are speaking.

Story time: Whenever I am talking to people about communication, they almost always seem to mention something about their weakness of saying too many "uhs," "ums," or "you knows." It is obvious that an ex-teacher got inside their head about it. I really want to tell them that their public speaking teacher was wrong, and that it is really not that big of a deal to say those things every now and then. I do not want to destroy their positive opinion of their old teacher, though. Not unless they ask me for help.

*TIP #133: Smile at your audience at the beginning of your presentations.

Smiling at the beginning of your presentations shows your audience that you are on their side. It is a great way to connect with them.

DO: Smile at your audience right before you start talking when you speak publicly.

DON'T: Smile too big or too fake.

There is something about starting out with positive energy that can calm your nerves and subtly communicate to your audience that you are about to give them something good.

Be careful: I included a warning about not being fake with your smile because it may come across as insincere, and maybe even a little weird.

Story time: I have noticed that smiling right before I begin public speaking almost has a magical kind of power. It immediately gets me in the right mind-set of being on the same side as the audience, not someone begging for their approval or afraid of being disliked.

*TIP #134: Don't assume your audience thinks your content is as interesting as you do.

I see so many speakers talk as if they think everyone already likes their topic. They seemingly do not do anything to try to make it more interesting whatsoever. This is a big mistake.

DO: Structure your presentation as if your audience is not interested in it yet.

DON'T: Assume everyone in your audience wants to hear what you have to say.

You should always consider the fact that there may be people in the audience who do not like your topic at all, and maybe don't even like you. Be sure you consider that possibility when you are preparing the content and make it as interesting as possible.

Assuming that the subject of your presentation is already embraced by your audience can make it come across as dry and boring. You may think the information is so great that it speaks for itself, but there is a good chance that not everyone agrees with you about that. Even if you are in a room full of your biggest fans who you would think would be interested in your content, you should still try to make your presentation enjoyable.

It may be true that you love your topic and think it is the coolest thing in the world, but that does not mean everybody will (at least not immediately) think that. You don't have to overdo it and put on a big, splashy, dramatic performance. Just realize that some members of the audience may have to be shown why your topic is awesome before they like it as much as you do.

*TIP #135: Don't depend on your slides during a presentation.

One common mistake that speakers often make is having too much dependence on slides. It is certainly okay to use them; just be sure they are an aide for you and not a crutch.

DO: Use slides if you think they would enhance your presentation.

DON'T: Be too dependent on your slides if you do use them.

Relying too much on your slides during a presentation can make you lose credibility with your audience because it makes you look like either you don't know what you are talking about or you are afraid.

The first step to using slides appropriately is to limit the number of them that you use. In most cases, no more than seven to ten or so is a good amount. Also, be sure you keep the words on your slides to a minimum (ten or twenty-five words at most). One benefit of this strategy is that when you know that you won't have many words on the screen while you are talking, you will hopefully force yourself to prepare a little better. This will save you from the temptation to turn your back on your audience while you read sentences that they can already see.

*TIP #136: Do not make presentations in professional situations the same way you did when you were in school.

Public speaking in professional environments is different than it is in an education setting. Be sure that you structure your presentations to fit the situation.

DO: Have a goal to make your presentations interesting for a general audience.

DON'T: Create presentations for a group of professionals the same way that you would have when you were in school.

When you had to give a presentation in school, it was mostly about the content. You were speaking for the benefit of teachers who had the power to give you a grade. They were judging you based on your ability to share content, not engage an audience.

Your motivation should be different when you are speaking publicly to a group of professional-type people. In those settings, your target audience is not one person but the entire population of the room. That means you need to consider what will make it interesting, entertaining, or useful for *that* group. Your focus should always be on who you are speaking to and what you are trying to do for them.

Be careful: There are exceptions to this advice, of course. If you are talking about something technical or highly detailed for a group of experts, then you may be better off just delivering the cold, hard facts. In most other settings, though, you should try your best to make your presentations both informative AND enjoyable.

Chapter 10

Communication and Social Skills for Your Job Search

Communication skills are an important part of any job search. Be sure you are giving yourself your best chance to find the best opportunity possible.

*TIP #137: Do not wait for jobs to be advertised before you ask about openings.

Sometimes the best jobs are never even advertised. That means you may have to use some social skills to find the less publicized ones.

DO: Ask about possible job openings, even if you don't see them listed.

DON'T: Assume that every job is posted online.

Now that many jobs are advertised online, some employers do not even make their best openings public. They know they can get a lot of unqualified candidates applying for jobs listed on the internet, and they would rather not deal with this annoyance. If you know what kind of job you are interested in, you cannot afford to be afraid to cold call, cold email, or walk into places and ask if they have any openings.

Online job searching can be helpful when you are looking for work; just do not make it your *only* strategy. Face-to-face methods can still be successful and are sometimes necessary to get the job you really want.

*TIP #138: Be friendly during job interviews.

You should obviously do your best to be as professional as possible during job interviews, but that does not mean you have to be uptight.

DO: Be friendly and act comfortable during job interviews.

DON'T: Get *too* casual and friendly.

The best approach for job interviews is to take them seriously but not *too* seriously. At the end of the day, it would be nice to be hired, but it is not going to be the end of the world if it does not work out. You should try to find a good balance between showing that you care about the job and not looking too desperate.

Be careful: Any time I give advice to loosen up during a serious situation, I have to include a reminder to not take it too far. You do not want to look intimidating, but you also should not come across too casual either. Just be friendly and act "normal," and you will have a much better chance of getting that job.

Story time: Soon after I graduated from college, I interviewed for a job that I was not very qualified for. To be honest I was not even close to having the resume for it. I still believed in myself, though, and thought that I would be a good hire for them. Despite the weaknesses on my resume, I did so well that the interviewer said that I reminded him of his son! I guess that was a good thing because I got the job. Interviews are about a lot more than just sharing your credentials. Making a personal connection can go a long way.

*TIP #139: During job interviews, calm your nerves by having a mindset that you are interviewing them too.

Interviews can be one of the most stressful things we do. One way to overcome the anxiety they cause is to remind yourself that you are not powerless in the situation.

DO: Ask questions during job interviews to help yourself overcome anxiety.

DON'T: Overdo it with *too* many questions.

Asking questions during job interviews will not only help you learn important information, but it can help your confidence too. You do not want to give the impression that you are weak and begging for approval. Instead, consider yourself a potential asset to the company that is deciding if you want to share your gifts with them.

The next time you have a job interview, remind yourself to truly *believe* that they would be lucky to have you. If you do not think that is true, then do not apply. You should not be excessive and ask them fifty questions, of course, but asking just two or three works just fine. You will find that you will not only have a lot more peace with this mindset, but you will be more confident too. That is a great attitude to have during any interview.

Chapter 11

Networking

Communication skills are an absolute must if you want to network to make professional connections. Whether you are going to organized networking events or just doing it randomly during your daily life, there are things you can do to help your cause.

NETWORKING EVENTS

*TIP #140: Do not stay with one person for more than a few minutes at networking events.

The best networkers talk to as many people as possible at networking events, only slowing down if there is a good reason. Even when that happens, you still might be better off continuing the conversation another time.

DO: Talk to as many people as possible at networking events.

DON'T: Move on from conversations before you first find out if there is potential for a good connection.

Being able to start and end conversations quickly is a valuable skill. Networking events can be a great opportunity for making new business contacts, but it helps if you can make the most of them talk to a lot of people. Once you figure out how to do that, you should find networking events at least as valuable as traditional methods of connecting like cold calling, knocking on doors, and advertising. This is not to say that you should stop doing these things and only focus on networking, just that you should consider including it in your business development strategy.

If you want to be able to talk to a lot of people at networking events, you need to get to the point quickly. You shouldn't overdo it and be in such a hurry that you rush through conversations, but even being aware of the amount of time you are spending with everyone can help you meet more people.

Be careful: This is not a suggestion to simply run a numbers game at networking events and pat yourself on the back for talking to a certain number of people. You still want your conversations to be productive, even if they are short. The key is being able to be quick but still have a purpose (and not look like a jerk in the process). Work on perfecting these things, and you will become a networking machine.

*TIP #141: Move on from conversations when there is no interest or connection at networking events.

As the saying goes, don't beat a dead horse. If you go to a networking event that has more than a few people in attendance, there is a good chance that you will not be able to talk to every single person there. So, it should make sense to try to be efficient with your time and end conversations that are clearly not going anywhere.

DO: Leave conversations quickly at networking events that are not productive.

DON'T: Let yourself get stuck in a conversation that you wish you could get out of.

If one of your goals at networking events is to talk to as many people as possible, you should end conversations when it is clear that there is not much going on. Maybe it is obvious that you will not be doing business together, or maybe the best next step with that person is just to exchange contact information. Whatever the reason is for keeping it short, you should not feel bad about wanting to leave. You should be respectful about the way you go about it, of course, but there is no reason to feel stuck.

If you have a hard time getting out of conversations, the key to doing it smoothly is to use transitional statements (like the ones discussed for personal situations in tip #86). Saying things like "nice to meet you" or "good seeing you again" or "do you have a card?" acts like a bridge to the next stage (saying goodbye) of the conversation. Transitional phrases make it clear you are hinting that the conversation is over without having to say so directly. That makes it less awkward for both sides. If someone is not picking up on your clues, then you may have to get more direct and say something like "I am going to go talk to some other people now." Do your best to try to exit gracefully first, though.

> Story time: When I first started going to networking events, I would get stuck in conversations with people for thirty minutes or longer and not be able to talk to many people as a result. I did not know how to get away. Now that I have learned a few techniques for saying goodbye, I am freer to talk to people for as long or as briefly as I want. I now have the power to end conversations without being awkward or insulting about it.

*TIP #142: If networking and other business events might help you, go to them even when you do not feel like it.

There may be times when you do not really want to go to a business event, but you still think it might be beneficial. Maybe you had a long day at work or maybe something in your personal life is stressing you out. But you should still go. You never know who you might meet who could change your life or your business.

DO: Go to networking events even when you do not feel like it.

DON'T: Be lazy or make excuses for not going to them.

Whenever you are not motivated to go to a networking event, it might help to remind yourself of the potential benefits they can have. There may be an opportunity for you to find work, get a client, or make connections that could be beneficial in the future. Unless you are sick or it is just not possible to go, motivate yourself to attend if you can. Maybe you will make a great connection there or maybe you won't. One thing is for sure, though, that if you stay home, your chances of meeting anyone will be zero. Networking events are potentially very valuable. Go! Go! Go!

*TIP #143: Dress well for networking events but not TOO well.

You may think that networking events are always a little stuffy. This is not usually true. Most of them could probably be described as professional but not formal, so you should wear something that fits that kind of environment.

DO: Dress professionally at networking events, but not too formally.

DON'T: Dress too casually just so you can "be yourself."

When you are going to a business event, a good general rule is to dress as if you just came from work (unless you work outside or do something that makes you dirty, obviously). This is not something you need to overthink. "Nice but not too nice" pretty much covers it. Networking events are not the time to dress in your t-shirt and shorts just because you want to be true to yourself. It is also not the time to dress extra formally because you want to impress people.

Every time you are in a professional setting, you are representing both yourself and your place of business. It is a good thing to remember when you are deciding what to wear to events where you might see people from your business community.

*TIP #144: Take steps to fight bad breath at networking events.

Bad breath can be so much of a turn-off that it can cost you business, so try not to let it keep you from making a good first impression.

DO: Be sure you are hydrated before and during networking events.

DON'T: Drink coffee, soda, or alcohol if you have not had plenty of water before the event.

The classic answer for bad breath is, of course, mints. They can be a temporary solution if you need to fix your breath quickly, but nothing helps you avoid bad breath better than staying hydrated. Other natural remedies for bad breath include strawberries, blueberries, and cinnamon.

Be careful: I am not saying you should never have coffee, soda, alcohol, or other drinks at networking events. A lot of times they are free, so they can be hard to pass up! Just be sure you have had enough water before or during the event and you can probably get away with other bad breath mistakes. The people to whom you are talking will appreciate it.

*TIP #145: Do not think of every interaction as pass/fail at networking events.

This is one of the universal social skills tips for all situations in this book, but it applies even more to networking events. Instead of trying to figure out how to overcome failure, it is better to shift your mindset to *totally eliminate the possibility of it.*

DO: Think of conversations at networking events as a search for good business connections, not a chance to pass or fail.

DON'T: Consider it a failure if someone does not like you or your business.

When you view every interaction at a networking event as a potential win/lose scenario, you put enormous pressure on yourself. Every time you talk to someone without making a sale or getting a client, there is a temptation to beat yourself up for failing. When you think like this, as soon as you are unsuccessful two or three times, you will probably feel bad about yourself and want to leave. It does not have to be this way.

No matter what your goal is for networking, whether it is getting clients, making sales, finding a job, or something else, you have not failed if you are not successful with everyone you talk to. When your goal is to make connections, there will inevitably be a certain number of people who will connect well with you for whatever reason and a certain number who will not. Once you accept this reality, you can handle the unsuccessful ones much more easily.

All you have really done when you do not get anywhere during a conversation is find someone in the category of people who is not a good connection for you or your business. So be it! That group of people exists for everyone. Instead of thinking of it as a failure when you do not click with someone, consider it, instead, as gained information. All you have done is found out that the person you talked to will probably not want to talk to you again. Good to know. This may take a complete change in mindset for you, but it helps tremendously once the idea sinks in.

The fear of failure can be crippling. Once you eliminate the pass/fail from even being a possibility, you can be much more at ease to search for connections without the fear of it not working out every time. There is no such thing as failure anymore with this mindset. You have removed it from the equation.

Story time: I used to be anxious about networking events, but once I changed my mindset to taking failure out of the picture, my comfort level at these events shot through the roof! I once met someone who said they had to psyche themselves up in the mirror before coming to networking events. I am comfortable at these events, so it surprised me to hear someone say that. It makes sense, though. Different people struggle with different things. Some people have to get themselves motivated to do public speaking from a stage, and some people have to do it for social situations. Different settings cause anxiety for different people. If you know that networking events could potentially help you or your business, don't worry about the people who aren't a good fit. Just be glad for the ones you meet who are.

*TIP #146: Pretend that you are already friends with everyone you meet at networking events.

This is another one of the universal social skills tips for all situations that applies even more so at networking events. If you want to be more likable and comfortable with them, you should treat people as though you already like them as soon as you meet.

DO: Imagine that you are already friends with new people you meet at networking events.

DON'T: Stop being friendly if it looks like there is no business connection.

This advice is especially useful because it not only helps you be more likable and therefore more successful, but it can improve your social comfort as well. When you imagine that you are already friends with whomever you are meeting, you come across as friendly and genuine. It can also help calm your nerves because there is no reason to be nervous or worried about whether that person will like you. People who already know and like each other do not feel like they have to be impressive to be liked, right? It's a great little mental trick.

It is always possible, of course, that you meet someone who *does not* want to be your friend and may even be icy or dismissive toward you, no matter how friendly you act toward them. This is nothing to be afraid of. There is no person that everyone likes and no business that everyone needs. If it happens, just accept it as something that happens to everyone, and you will not have a reason to feel any stress over it.

Be careful: If you find out that there is not much of a connection with someone or this person is not interested in your business, don't let it bother you. It is okay to just move on. All you did was gain the information that this person is not a great connection which is no big deal. There is something freeing about taking total control of your self-esteem like this. When you focus on treating people well before you know how they will treat you, it is much easier to be at ease in social situations—even formal business ones.

*TIP #147: Don't be afraid to approach any size group of people at networking events.

If you ever go to larger networking events, you will probably notice that there are groups of all sizes. You will see groups of two and sometimes three or more. There may even occasionally be one person standing alone. If you want to be a great networker, you can't let the size of the group stop you from approaching.

DO: Be willing to walk up to anyone in any size group at a networking event.

DON'T: Force your way into conversations of any sized group if it looks like they are having an intense discussion.

One of the great things about networking events is that everybody knows the goal of the event. People are expecting strangers to talk to them, enter into their conversations, and so on, so there is no reason to feel weird about walking up to people. The risk of social awkwardness compared to a random situation is dramatically reduced.

Just be prepared for the chance that you may not be welcomed into a group if they already have a serious conversation going on. If that happens, you should not feel bad if they do not invite you into the discussion. It is important to realize that it is not a reflection of you. When you do run into a situation where you are not welcomed into the conversation, the one thing you *should not* do is try to force your way in. Just accept that it is not the best group to try to join and look for another one.

Be careful: I think the best thing to do at networking events is to first look for people who are standing alone. If there is nobody solo, you can then look for larger groups to join. This advice is more of a guideline than a rule, though. Once you get comfortable going to these kinds of events, you will get good at figuring out which groups of people are the best ones to try to join.

*TIP #148: Don't automatically avoid networking events with high ticket prices.

It is a big mistake to avoid networking events because of the entry cost, within reason. The money you save by only going to the free/cheaper ones is not worth the opportunities that you will be missing to make great connections.

DO: Go to as many networking events as you can, including ones that have an entry fee.

DON'T: Rule out networking events just because there is a cost for attending, even if they are a little expensive.

When you go to free events, chances are probably higher that you will meet people on a tight budget like you are. If you go to an event that has an entry fee, there are more likely to be people there who are in higher positions in their company and therefore making more money. These may not be the only kinds of people who you want to meet, but you definitely don't want to exclude them.

If your goal is just to connect with professionals in general, the cheaper events probably make the most sense for you. If you want to make connections with people who can hire you or do business with you, the more expensive events are likely your best shot.

Be careful: This is not to say you should rule out free events and assume there will be nobody at them worth meeting. I have made some great connections at the free events too. If you think about the big picture like I do, the people who are looking for work now may still be a good business connection in the future. Just realize that the higher-profile people in your town are more likely to go to the more serious events.

Story time: Despite my lack of funds early on in my networking experience, I changed my strategy of exclusively going to free events after talking to an experienced networker. He inspired me to change my approach when he told me that events that have a ticket price are sometimes the best ones to go to. This advice might sound backward, but there is a lot of wisdom in it. My fellow networker said that the people who go to events that cost a little extra may just be the type of people you want to meet. If the event is free, you are going to meet people who go to free events. If you go to events that have an entry fee, you are going to meet people who can afford to pay for them—like managers, owners, and other decision-making types. From then on, I made a point to start going to the nonfree events more often.

*TIP #149: Do not smother people at networking events.

No matter how badly you want to succeed, you should be careful not to be a nuisance to people at networking events.

DO: Do your best to be successful at networking events.

DON'T: Smother people in the process of trying to be successful at them.

Being too needy can make you smother the very people who can help you the most. "Smothering" means that you act like you are obsessed with winning them over without considering their interests or point of view. This happens at a networking event when someone keeps going with their pitch even after they make it clear that they do not want to do business with you. It's rude and it can create an extremely uncomfortable situation.

Be careful: As I mentioned in other tips, networking should be a process of looking for connections and then making your pitch if it appears that a person is interested. You do not want to be the type who gets pushy and relentless with people whether they show interest or not. You will quickly get a bad reputation and maybe even banned from events if you take this approach.

*TIP #150: Don't take too much time talking to people you already know at networking events.

It is often impossible to talk to everyone at large events, so time efficiency is important.

DO: Say hello to friends and connections you have already made at networking events.

DON'T: Talk to people you have known for very long at networking events.

This is not to suggest that you be rude and totally ignore your friends and acquaintances you see at networking events, but be aware that the clock is ticking. Every minute that you talk to someone you know is a minute that you are not able to talk to someone new.

This rule is more of a general guide than one you necessarily have to stick to 100 percent of the time. Sometimes it might actually be more beneficial to talk longer to deepen a relationship with someone you already know. Just be sure you are strategic about how you go about it. Talking to your friends just because it is more comfortable is not a good use of your time. You can always talk to your friends somewhere else later, but great networking opportunities are not always easy to find.

Story time: I remember the first time I ever went to a networking event. A friend of mine told me about it, and I wanted to give one a try. I went in for a few minutes, and I do not think I talked to one person I did not know. My friend and I sat down, and I talked to him for the rest of the night. We could have done that anywhere at any time! I eventually learned that I needed to be a little more intentional about how I spent my time at networking events.

*TIP #151: If networking events cause you extreme anxiety, go somewhere on your way to them to talk to a stranger to warm up.

Networking events can cause just as much anxiety for some people as public speaking does for others. If this is true for you, there are little things you can do to help make yourself more comfortable. A simple warm up can do a lot to get you calmed down before going to the actual event.

DO: Practice talking to strangers in nonthreatening situations before you go to networking events. This can help you get more comfortable.

DON'T: Feel like it is impossible to overcome your networking event anxiety.

Networking events trigger anxiety for some people. They may be looking for a new job, a new client, or new business connections. That can be intimidating!

If you have social anxiety in general, one fairly easy way to help you begin to overcome it is to practice in low-stress situations. Once you do that a few times, it is not such a big leap to go into more pressure-filled settings. For example, the next time you are planning on going to a networking event, you might want to try going to a grocery store on the way over and having a quick conversation with the person in the checkout line or the person bagging your groceries. That will give you a low-pressure chance to practice small talk. This may seem like a silly exercise to someone who does not have social anxiety, but doing little things like this to warm up can make a big difference if this is a problem you face. Even better, practice your small-talk skills whenever you get a chance during your everyday life. It does not have to be limited to the days that you are attending events.

Be careful: I have met people who think there is something wrong with them if they get nervous going to networking events. There is no reason to think that way! We all have things that make us anxious, so don't beat yourself up over it. If networking events happen to be your weakness, so be it. What matters is that you don't let the anxiety stop you from going to them if you think they could benefit you.

*TIP #152: Do not flirt or joke inappropriately at business events.

Networking events are not the place to be on the search for romance. Even if you are just joking with people, be sure you do not cross the line and use humor inappropriately.

DO: Feel free to joke and kid with people at business events.

DON'T: Joke about anything that can be taken as sexual or offensive in any way.

You may think that networking events would be a great place to meet someone to date. There are usually a lot of intelligent, successful, and friendly people at them. That is obviously not what they are designed for, though. If you go to these events with the intention of trying to find romance, you run the risk of making a fool of yourself, being embarrassed, or even getting banned.

Making people laugh is a lot of fun, and humor can be a great way to connect with people you meet. That does not mean that you should cross the line of inappropriateness to do it. There is a fine line between being funny and being offensive, so take that line seriously. You don't have to be on eggshells and never joke with people out of fear of accidentally being offensive; just be wise about how you go about it. Being known as the guy who hits on women at business events would not be good for your reputation.

Be careful: I am not saying you are a terrible person if you meet someone great at a networking event and start dating them. I am sure it has happened before. The point of this advice is to be sure that flirting is not your main objective. If you do find romance at a networking event, it should be almost accidental.

*TIP #153: Take no for an answer at networking events.

Making new contacts through networking events is more personal than other situations. That means you should be a little more careful about potentially offending people than you might usually be.

DO: Try your best to make connections at networking events.

DON'T: Keep pushing people to buy or connect with you if they have already said no.

This is not to suggest that you should be rude or pushy in other situations. It is just that meeting people at networking events is in its own category with its own etiquette. Not only are these events more personal, but there is a good chance that you could see the same people over and over again at future events. You do not want to insult people whom you are going to see that often or establish a bad reputation for yourself.

If someone is clearly not interested in talking to you or doing business with you, accept it and move on. There are probably plenty of other people there whom you can talk to. Save your "not taking no for an answer" approach for other settings.

*TIP #154: Do not be afraid to stand alone at networking events.

Standing by yourself for a few minutes at a networking event is no big deal.

DO: Stand alone if you do not see anyone available to talk to at a networking event.

DON'T: Stand by yourself for too long.

People sometimes say that they do not go to networking events because there is a good chance that they will not know anyone there. They think they would feel uncomfortable with approaching groups of people who are already talking and they would also feel strange about standing alone. None of these concerns should stop you from going! There are multiple tips in this book about strategies for approaching strangers, but standing alone sometimes can be helpful too.

First of all, standing by yourself shows confidence. You are demonstrating that you do not have to be talking to someone to feel good about yourself. If you are concerned about looking weird or being uncomfortable, you might want to try finding something to lean on, like a bar or counter, so you are not just standing in the middle of the room by yourself. If there is no place to lean on something, you can at least stand close to a wall. There is nothing wrong with being a wallflower if that is what makes you feel at ease. That would be a lot better than staying at home!

Be careful: You probably should not stand by yourself forever. If you do it for more than a few minutes, you might want to start walking around the room and trying to join other conversations. At the very least, change locations. It is one thing to stand by yourself for a minute or two in the same place; if you do it all night without moving, at that point you might start to look a little strange.

*TIP #155: Do not avoid networking events where you do not seem to fit in.

Some networking events advertise for specific groups of people. There are events that target women, tech professionals, HR people, CEOs, realtors, and just about every other group you can think of. Unless it is absolutely clear that you are excluded, though, you should not hesitate to go.

DO: Go to as many networking events as possible, even when they do not seem to fit your demographic.

DON'T: Go to events where you are not welcome.

Most networking events are open to the general public. Even if they have some kind of designated group that they highlight, they probably are not doing so at the exclusion of everyone else. These are the kinds of events you should attend even if you do not exactly fit the targeted group. If you are not sure if it would be appropriate to go to certain events, you can always get in touch with the organizers of the event and ask.

One of your goals for networking should be to connect with as many businesspeople as possible in your community. That includes people who are different from you, which means going where different kinds of people go.

Story time: One of my networking role models would often ask me if I had gone to a particular event. Sometimes I would answer—no, that event was for _____ (fill in a demographic that I did not fit into). He would inevitably roll his eyes and laugh and tell me that I could still have gone. He taught me that I should not exclude myself from events where it would have probably been acceptable for me to go to.

*TIP #156: Do not make assumptions about networking events and the people who attend them.

People have all kinds of different opinions about networking events and the people who go to them. Some of the opinions are valid, but many are not realistic.

DO: Keep an open mind about people who go to networking events.

DON'T: Generalize about the kinds of people who go to them.

People avoid going to networking events for all kinds of reasons. Some say they do not like the salesy types of people who go to them, or they think they are a waste of time, or something else. What is strange about these comments is that these people have often never actually *been* to an organized networking event! They are basing their opinions on assumptions, what other people have told them, or, at best, on one or two experiences.

Yes, some of these complaints may be valid for some networking events, but most of them are full of friendly, receptive people. Of course, there is going to be *some* element of sales and self-promotion at them—that is what they were created for. As long as you know and accept this going in, though, you can often find networking events to be a very useful (and enjoyable) way to make business connections.

Be careful: While I do love networking events, I am not suggesting that they are for everyone. If you have a bad experience after a bad experience, you probably should not go anymore. Maybe you have a job that does not require lead generation, so they aren't directly useful for you (although I still think it is a good idea to make connections in your local business community). If you are truly the kind of person who is not cut out for networking events, there is no reason to force yourself. Just do not come to that conclusion without giving them a real chance.

> Story time: When I first started going to networking events, I had no idea what to expect. I knew a few people who went to them occasionally, but other than hearing a little about their experience, I did not know what they would be like. What I found (in my town, at least) was that mostly everyone at these events was extremely friendly and casual. There was no reason for me to be intimidated or worried about how I would be treated.

*TIP #157: Have big-picture goals at networking events.

If your only objective at networking events is to get immediate business, you are setting yourself up for stress, excessive pressure, and failure. Not only that, you are going to annoy a lot of people.

DO: Have a clear idea about your goals for networking events before you show up to them.

DON'T: Limit them to short-term goals only.

If you go to a networking event and do not meet a single person to do business with, it is still a success. How is that possible? Because you still made connections or at the very least made people in the business community more familiar with you.

Having big-picture goals like this can also help you overcome the social anxiety that networking events can cause. When big-picture success is your objective, there is much less pressure on individual interactions.

Story time: I have had people tell me that they met me months ago (or longer) at a networking event, and now they are ready to do business with me. Networking success is not just measured by immediate results. The most successful people play the long game. They know that some business relationships take time to develop. You never know how a random connection today might turn into something great in the future.

RANDOM NETWORKING

*TIP #158: Always be ready to give your thirty-second pitch.

If you have a job that requires meeting people and making new contacts, your thirty-second pitch (or elevator pitch) is crucial. If you can't say what you do quickly and clearly, you might miss out on opportunities when time to talk is limited.

DO: Plan out your thirty-second pitch ahead of time.

DON'T: Wing it.

Do not underestimate the value of being able to tell people about yourself and your business in a short amount of time. Yes, it is possible to make connections in other ways like cold calling, advertising, and social media, but why waste opportunities to do it face to face too?

If you want to be good at giving elevator pitches, you should be well prepared before you get into those situations. If you make up your elevator pitch on the fly, you may not be able to communicate your message clearly enough.

Your goal when creating your thirty-second pitch should be to make it simple enough so that a child could understand it. Your quick pitch is no time to get fancy. You should try to be able to express what you do quickly and clearly so that people decide right then if they might want to do business with you. Simplicity and getting to the point are the keys to being able to do this well.

*TIP #159: Do not give your business card out immediately when meeting someone new.

The timing of when you give people your business card during a conversation makes a difference.

DO: Give out your business card *after* it becomes clear that you have a connection of some kind with people.

DON'T: Give out your card as soon as you start talking to someone.

Networking should be about making connections, not just pushing your contact information on everyone you meet. When you hand out your business card immediately, you are doing the same thing as email spamming. There is no attempt to find out if a person is a good connection or even if they are interested in your business—you are just shoving your information at them. Nobody likes to be spammed.

Giving out your business card when you first meet someone networking is like giving out your phone number as soon as you meet a woman you want to date. It signals desperation and a lack of social awareness. Wouldn't you first want to find out if you are interested in the woman and if she is interested in you? The same goes for business connections. Do not assume people want your card before they find out if you might be a good connection first.

This mistake may not seem like that big a deal, but people notice this kind of thing. Randomly giving out your card to as many people as possible may sound like a smart numbers game, but it is not a winning strategy. It should be more of a discerning process, finding out if people could benefit from knowing you and *then* exchanging contact information.

It may take a little more effort to network this way, but it is worth the effort. People will appreciate it when you do not just immediately throw your card at them. Those are the cards that are usually the first ones to go into the trash.

Story time: I have never seen this happen before or since, but at one networking event I was attending there was a guy who was walking around just handing out business cards. He did not even stop to talk! He just walked up and gave his card and moved on. At least most people who start by giving their cards stay around and talk to you after they do. This guy is a rare case, but you still don't want to be someone who gives out their card too early in the conversation.

*TIP #160: Be aware of people's body language and other signals when you are networking (just don't overread them).

Most people are not blunt enough to just say exactly what they are thinking. That does not mean we should not try to figure it out, though.

DO: Be aware of body language that might signal what people are thinking about you and the conversation you are having.

DON'T: Assume you can be 100 percent sure about what different types of body language mean.

It is extremely difficult to network successfully if you do not take the time to try to understand other people's points of view. Maybe they are interested in hiring you or working with you. Or maybe they are hoping they can end the conversation as soon as possible and never talk to you again. It would obviously be useful to know this kind of information.

So, what is the best way to figure these things out if people do not make it obvious? The answer is reading body language. Are they engaged in the conversation or do they look around the room as if they are looking for someone better to talk to? Are they leaning away from you or even stepping away like there is a magnet trying to pull them out of the conversation? These are just a few of the signals that could reveal someone's true level of interest in the conversation.

Be careful: Yes, it can be very helpful to read body language, but it can also backfire if you read it incorrectly. If you misread the meaning of a certain kind of body language, you could mistakenly believe that someone is thinking something they are not. That could cause a huge misunderstanding if you take action based on what you assume is true without being sure.

The study of body language can be very useful. Pay attention to signs that probably mean something, but don't think you have some magic trick that helps you read people's minds perfectly. It is not an exact science by any means. For example, the classic body language case of folding your arms does not always mean people are closed off or not interested. It could also just mean they are cold! Think of body language as something that can give us clues but rarely definite answers.

We can't always be positive about what body language means, but we should still pay attention to it. Whether it is body language or just a vibe that we are feeling, we should always try to be aware of how we are affecting others. Commit to only pursuing the connections who already show signs of interest and you will have a much higher rate of success. You will be more likable too.

*TIP #161: Be memorable when making a first impression.

Sometimes being remembered is more important than being good.

DO: Think of ways to make yourself and/or your business stand out from everyone else.

DON'T: Be memorable for the wrong reasons.

There are many ways to be memorable, and they are not always positive. You can be remembered for being great at something, and you can be memorable for being different or charming. Or you can also stand out for something negative. You obviously shouldn't do anything foolish to be remembered, but you should still try to figure out a way to be noticed.

If you network a lot, being memorable is important. You may be one of the hundreds of people a person meets on a given day. So, what can you do to stand out from the crowd? If you make a good impression, you obviously want it to stick.

Maybe you could think of an interesting way to tell your story, or you could explain how you are better than the competition in some way. You may even have a quirk that is unforgettable. There are many ways to accomplish this. You may need to get creative if you can't think of a good way to separate yourself from the competition.

If you are struggling to figure out a way to make yourself be remembered in person, you should, at least, try to make yourself memorable online somehow. Even just posting regularly on your social media is a step in the right direction. Anything to avoid being easily forgotten is a plus.

Story time: I once talked to a guy at a networking event who said that he remembered talking to me TWO YEARS prior and now wanted to possibly do business. Wow! That made me wonder what I was doing that stood out so much. Maybe it is my friendly nature or maybe it is my bald head. Who knows. Maybe it is because my business is a little outside of the box. Whatever the reason, I want to make more of an effort to be intentional about being memorable when I meet new people in business settings. Even if the thing that makes you stand out is not business related, it is still beneficial to be remembered.

*TIP #162: Send a message within twenty-four hours of getting contact info when you are networking.

Networking can be hard work, even if you love it. So, don't waste all your effort by losing touch with your new connections. Make it a priority to reach out by the next day at the latest so you can keep the conversation fresh.

DO: Follow up quickly with people you meet at networking events.

DON'T: Follow up *too* quickly.

Some people you talk to when you are networking may have met fifty new people or more that day, so getting in touch with them very soon may be your only chance to be remembered. This is especially true if you did not talk to them for very long. Be sure you take this seriously, because you never know who might be a valuable connection.

Be careful: Even though it is important that you get in touch quickly with someone you just met, make sure you do not go overboard with your messaging speed. If you meet someone and then text that person ten minutes later, for instance, you might look a little pushy or desperate. That is a little TOO fast. In most cases, it is a good idea to play it cool and reach out to new contacts the next day. Being in the habit of following up fast, but not annoyingly fast, will give you the best chance of making your connections strong from the beginning.

*TIP #163: Make introductions to help others connect.

Helping people without asking for anything in return is what good people do.

DO: Try to introduce people you think would benefit from knowing each other.

DON'T: Get so focused on connecting others that you lose sight of your own goals for networking.

When you are networking, do not just focus on looking for leads for yourself. Try to make connections for other people as well and you will often be rewarded in some way. Even if you don't get directly rewarded, you will still be making a contribution to your business communication, and that is always a plus.

Part of the business karma strategy that was mentioned earlier includes getting people together who may help each other. People remember when you do something to help them, especially if you do not ask for anything back.

Even if you never get direct benefit out of it, at least you have done something good, right? You are rewarded either way.

Be careful: Making connections for other people is a great thing to do; just be sure you do not get so carried away with it that you forget to work on your own goals as well. A good balance of helping others while not forgetting to look out for yourself as well is a good recipe for long-term success.

*TIP #164: Get advice from older, experienced networkers about their methods.

No matter how good you get at networking, you can never know it all. It makes sense to try to learn from other people who have more experience than you.

DO: Seek out advice from people who have been going to networking events for a long time.

DON'T: Take advice from just anyone.

Many older people love helping younger people, especially when they show an interest in learning about their area of expertise. Some of them may have been networking for fifty years! Now that is the kind of person that is great to learn from.

Be careful: Do not just take advice from any older person you talk to. Being older is not always a guarantee of being wiser. If you do not know very much about someone's character and past, you should be careful about trusting them enough to take their advice. Some of it may do you more harm than good.

Once you do find people with a lot of networking experience and you think they are worth listening to, try to learn as much as you can from them. Many of the fundamentals of networking and business in general have not changed much over the years.

*TIP #165: Try to get to the phrase "what do you do?" as quickly as possible when networking.

If you can't find out what kind of work people do, it will be impossible to know if they might be a good connection.

DO: Try to find out what kind of work people do ASAP when networking.

DON'T: Chitchat for so long with people that you never get around to asking what their job is.

Okay, so you have decided that you want to network, either at official networking events or at random places. But how should you go about it?

If you only remember one tip from this book about networking, this should be it. The main purpose of networking is to find out if a possible business connection exists. So you can't learn that information if you do not know what the other person does, right?

Some people are concerned that they might look weird if they ask someone what they do, but there is really no reason to have those fears. It is probably one of the *least* awkward things you could ask someone. People expect it, especially at networking and other types of business events. If you let a fear of embarrassment stop you from trying to network in random places, then you are just creating awkwardness in your head that does not have to be there. Most people either love to talk about their jobs or are dying to talk about how much they wish they were doing something else. Your question about what they do will likely be welcomed.

The "quickly" part in this tip is included because you never know how much time you are going to have to talk to someone. Do not assume that you will have people's attention for as long as you want it. If you wait too long to get to the "what do you do?" question, the conversation may end before you even get a chance to get around to it. Or, you may get off track talking about something else and forget to even bring it up. So, make it your goal to try to find out quickly.

Be careful: If you notice, I said your goal should be to ask what they do, not try to force what YOU do into the conversation. Pushing your own agenda too hard can make you look salesy and kill your chances of making a good impression. The good news is that when you ask people about their occupations, they will usually ask you about yours too! Boom. And what if they never get around to asking you what you do? So be it. They probably weren't really interested in making a connection with you anyway.

Story time: When I first started studying random networking, this was one of the missing pieces of the puzzle for me. I got to the point where I could easily start conversations with people, but I would often get distracted and forget to ask what their job was. Then I would be mad at myself after they got away without giving me their contact information without any knowledge of what they even did for work. This is why it is a good idea to have a networking plan and not have to think too much on the fly.

*TIP #166: Don't wait for official networking events to network.

Even if you live in a city where networking events are held regularly, you should still try to network in random situations during your day as well. Every extra person you talk to could be the one who dramatically improves your life or business.

DO: Be willing to network at both official networking events and in random places.

DON'T: Think networking events are the only place where you have "permission" to network.

Networking events are a great way to make connections because they are set up to make it easy to talk to people. Everyone there understands the purpose of the event, so you can eliminate a lot of the apprehension that can come from approaching strangers. Even if you have general social anxiety, that should not stop you from trying to network. The potential benefits are just too great. The people who attend these kinds of events can be intimidating, but there is really no need to be afraid of them.

Networking events are not the only way to make connections, though. You can and should be ready to do it 24/7. Some people seem to think it is awkward or weird to try to make business connections by talking to strangers, but it does not have to be. If you struggle with the thought of talking to people you don't know, go back and read some of the previous tips in this book about starting conversations, making small talk, and so on. It really is possible to talk to people casually and comfortably if you know how to go about it.

Whether you go to multiple networking events per week or if you go to zero, you should still include random networking as part of your business development strategy. Even if you do not have a specific purpose for networking, like looking for a job or clients, it is still a good idea to make connections in your city. That means there is always a reason to network. Be open to talking to people wherever you go, or you may miss out on some great opportunities. Places like coffee shops, bookstores, and other places where professional people hang out are the best places to do random networking. Any location could be a possible place to network.

The best methods for networking with strangers are similar to the strategies that were already discussed that you should use at official networking events. It is all about making a casual approach and then figuring out if there might be a good business connection there. If that looks like a possibility, you can then offer to exchange contact info and go from there. It is as simple as that. The good news is that you do not have to be an extrovert or a people person to be able to do this. These skills can be learned.

Story time: When I first started studying social skills, I tried to figure out how to do random networking with strangers before I ever even went to an organized networking event. I had no idea what to say when I first started doing it and I felt extremely awkward. But I kept at it. I would try to talk to people at coffee shops, standing and waiting for the streetlight to change, in actual elevators, and anywhere else I happened to be. As a result of all this practice, I have now reached a pretty high level of confidence and ability to network in any situation. It is not that difficult to master once you learn some basic strategies and get out and practice.

Chapter 12

General Communication and Social Skills Wisdom

Communication skills wisdom sometimes applies to certain situations and sometimes there are general strategies that fit anywhere.

*TIP #167: Be obsessed with self-awareness.

The better you know yourself, the better your chances are for finding success, happiness, and peace.

DO: Try to discover your strengths, weaknesses, interests, dislikes, and so on.

DON'T: Focus on the weaknesses and talents you do not have.

We all have strengths, weaknesses, likes, and dislikes, and some of them may be drastically different from other people. It is possible to improve some of these things, but there are others that are impossible to change. The more we become aware of which is which, the more we can figure out what we need to either work on or just accept.

Be careful: I use the word "obsessed" to describe how serious you should be about self-awareness because it is that important. If you don't know yourself, you are just kind of wandering through life and letting things happen to you when what you should really be doing is strategizing to give yourself your best chances for happiness and success. If you have not already been looking inward and assessing yourself, it is time to start studying yourself and getting to know what makes you tick.

*TIP #168. Don't judge people too harshly for bad behavior if their intent is good.

Sometimes people can make us mad when they actually meant well.

DO: Consider people's motives before you get too upset with them.

DON'T: Totally excuse people's bad behavior just because they meant well.

We should probably always pause and think before we get angry at someone for any reason, but this is especially true when it is clear that they had good intentions—even if we don't like what they did. This could include anything from giving us constructive criticism to doing something we don't like that doesn't involve us.

This is not to say that good intentions should be a free pass for bad behavior. Far from it. The point of this advice is just to slow down and consider people's motives as part of the entire picture before making a judgment about what they did.

Be careful: Getting offended can be exhausting. If you look hard enough, you can probably find something to be upset by any time you want to. If you think this way you can spend your entire life being vulnerable to the next unpleasant thing someone says or does. You are better off if you realize that many things that upset us don't really matter in the big picture. Whether the bad behavior comes from a stranger or someone you are close to, it is always wise to try to think about the motivation for their actions. This would be a good approach to take whenever we are insulted or offended by people.

*TIP #169: Do not compare yourself to others.

Jealousy is a waste of time and energy.

DO: Be grateful for who you are and what you have.

DON'T: Measure yourself against others in a way that makes you feel bad about yourself.

You should never beat yourself up or feel bad just because someone is better looking, has a better job, better stuff, and so on. If you want to use success as a motivator, that's one thing. Just do not let jealousy ruin your life.

The problem with jealousy is that you can never relax. There is no endpoint to it where you can finally be at ease and have peace of mind. If you are jealous about something material, there will always be something better and you will never have enough. If you are jealous of someone's relationship, you will never find a perfect one. Being in the habit of comparing yourself to others is a good way to have an unhappy life.

*TIP #170: Don't be embarrassed to go out solo.

It will not destroy your reputation if you go out on your own every now and then when you do not have anyone to go with you.

DO: Go out in public when you want to, regardless of whether you are alone or with others.

DON'T: Let the fear of being seen out alone stop you from doing things you want to do.

We give way too much attention to what other people think of us. This kind of thinking can completely steal your joy of living! As long as you are acting with character and class, you should feel free to do what you want to do and not worry about what people think about it. If they are judging you for something as stupid as going out by yourself, though, that is their problem, not yours.

Be careful: I should add a warning to this tip to not go out alone if you think it would put you in a dangerous situation. I am not suggesting that you throw common sense out the window and put yourself at risk. This advice is more about not deciding to stay at home just because you are afraid of being seen out by yourself and having people think you aren't cool.

*TIP #171: Be intentional about establishing a good reputation.

Your reputation is everything. Even if you do not have a job that depends on making contacts or working with the public, you never know when a good reputation can open doors for you. The reverse is true as well—you never know when a bad reputation might close doors.

DO: Consider how your actions, big and small, will affect your reputation.

DON'T: Be careless about how you act in public.

Everything you do in public can influence what people think of you. Be sure you consider how your actions will look to others, especially people who do not know you well. This is even more true now than it used to be with the potential to be videoed or photographed anywhere you go.

Be careful: I am not suggesting being fake just to score points with people. Just be aware of how you are acting when you are in public.

Story time: My grandfather had a great reputation in his town. He truly loved people and it showed. Yes, it was good for his job as an insurance salesman to be popular, but he acted like he was your friend whether you could help his business or not. People still talk about how much they liked him more than twenty years after he passed away. I try to follow his example.

*TIP #172: Regularly look for opportunities to sharpen your communication and social skills.

Even if you study every communication and social skills tip in existence, it still takes practice to become great. If you want to see noticeable improvement, you should take advantage of every opportunity you can find.

DO: Go out of your way to practice communication and social skills as much as possible.

DON'T: Assume you can learn great communication and social skills just from reading about them.

Communication and social skills are extremely valuable and necessary for success in many areas of life, so you would be wise to take them seriously. It may be a little inconvenient or stressful to get out of your comfort zone sometimes, but if you remind yourself of the potential benefits of improving these skills, it will be easier to motivate yourself to try to improve.

The whole world can be your social laboratory if you take advantage of it. Studying (like reading this book) can help, but it takes action and practice to really make a difference in your skills.

*TIP #173: Give a good handshake.

It seems like your handshaking style should not matter much, but it can. Believe it or not, some people are judging you based on it.

DO: Be sure that your grip is not too weak or too strong when you shake hands.

DON'T: Overcompensate with your grip or the number of times you shake just to prove that you have a strong handshake.

The way you shake hands matters. A strong handshake is not some kind of badge of honor, but some people overkill it as if they think the tighter the grip, the better the handshake. Going too far like that can make you look like a weirdo. There are others on the opposite end of the spectrum who seem to have no tension in their hands whatsoever. As long as you avoid either of these extremes, you are probably okay.

The only things you really need to know about shaking hands are to use slight firmness and take no more than a few seconds. This does not mean a good handshake alone will guarantee you success; it is just one of those first impression issues to be aware of.

Be careful: Whether you think it is fair to be judged by your handshake does not really matter. That is just how it is. You might be thinking, "I don't care what people think who judge others based on their handshakes." I understand the logic of this, but it is not big enough of a deal to burn bridges over. There are enough people who pay attention to this, so make sure you have a good one.

*TIP #174: Do not feel obligated to explain why you can't make plans with someone.

I have to take a stand against the common expectation that we must give a reason for turning down someone's invitation to socialize.

DO: Use general phrases like "I'm sorry, but I have plans" or "I'm so sorry, but I'm busy that night" when turning down an invitation to socialize with people.

DON'T: Feel obligated to explain *exactly why* you can't go somewhere with someone.

It is nothing short of arrogant for people to assume they have the right to make you explain why you are turning down an invitation to socialize with them. This seems to be a pretty common occurrence, though, and you may even do it yourself. Some people will keep pressing you to give them a reason even *after* you try to make it clear that you do not want to give them one. Ugh!

This advice applies to friends, family members, business associates, or anyone else who feels like they have a right to know why you say no to making plans with them. Don't let anyone in any situation pressure you to give a reason.

Not only should you not feel pressured to explain your reasons for telling someone no, but you should not even volunteer that information on your own either. One reason explaining yourself is a bad idea is that your explanation opens the door for the person to question the legitimacy of your reason. Then you are stuck. As soon as you start explaining why you are saying no, you are setting yourself up for a potential argument about why that is not a good enough excuse for canceling. Either that or you are risking hurting people's feelings when you explain why you would rather do your thing rather than their thing. It is best just to avoid either possibility and give a very general explanation like "sorry I have plans" or "sorry I have something scheduled for that time."

Also, it should go without saying that *you* should not be the person on the other side of this as well. Do not be the one who pushes other people to explain why they can't make plans with you when *your* invitations get turned down.

Be careful: I have to be careful with this advice because you could easily come across as rude if you do not choose your words wisely. I am not suggesting that you get angry or get an attitude when someone asks you to explain why you can't socialize. Just know that you have a right to keep your plans private if you want to.

*TIP #175: Be careful about drawing conclusions from people's words and actions.

Bad mind reading is one of the most destructive things that can happen to any relationship, whether it's personal or professional, lifelong or new.

DO: Pay attention to people's body language, signals, and words.

DON'T: Assume you know for certain what these things mean.

One of the biggest mistakes people make is assuming they *know for sure* how to draw perfect conclusions about what certain things mean, like body language, tone, and just general communication. You may be pretty good at reading people, but it is still usually a guess to some degree. No matter how good you are at observing and reading people, be sure that you don't assume that you are PERFECT at it. Looking for clues about what people are thinking is fine. Assuming you are always right and jumping to conclusions without much evidence can be a big mistake and have serious consequences.

Be careful: It is probably a mistake to assume that you can be sure that _____ means _____ (fill in the action and meaning that you are assuming is true). Reacting to people with the assumption that you know what they mean or think with 100 percent certainty can cause big problems. Be wise and consider the possibility that you could occasionally misunderstand.

*TIP #176: Don't walk with your head down.

Looking down while you walk is a bad idea for many reasons.

DO: Walk with your eyes looking straightforward.

DON'T: Walk with your eyes looking down.

Walking with your head down can make you look like you lack confidence. A good way to overcome this bad habit is to remind yourself to keep your eyes and chin pointing straight forward. After repeating this strategy a few times, it will become a habit and you won't even have to think about it anymore. This advice may not sound like it matters much, but it can make a difference. Anything you can do to make yourself more likable and approachable is a plus.

*TIP #177: Don't be an "eye contact avoiding zombie."

Some people are so afraid of social interactions that they do whatever they can to avoid them. One thing they often do is look away from people they pass by, with a cold stare in their eyes, looking like an "eye contact avoiding zombie."

DO: Try to make eye contact with people as you walk past them.

DON'T: Hold your eye contact for too long and make people uncomfortable.

Do not let the possibility of talking to strangers make you so uncomfortable that you avoid making eye contact with them at all costs. If you are in the habit of doing this, it is time to start taking steps to overcoming your extreme social discomfort.

"Eye contact avoiding zombies" are easy to spot. They walk around looking straight ahead like they are in a trance as they pass by. They do this because they do not want anyone walking past them to think it is okay to start a conversation with them. Yikes. Talk about living scared.

Talking to strangers is only a big deal if you make it a big deal. It is nothing to be afraid of, especially if you follow some of the strategies in this book to help make it more comfortable for you.

Be careful: I realize that in some cultures and regions, making eye contact might be taken as an insult. If you are in a place where that is the case, you should be careful about how and when you do it.

*TIP #178: Take the high road as much as possible.

There will be times in your life when you will be disrespected in some way. It is usually best not to fight fire with fire and trade insults in these situations.

DO: Respond to insults with kindness, a dismissive attitude, or nothing.

DON'T: Answer insults with some of your own.

Taking the high road means you do not answer insult for insult. When you are faced with disrespect of some kind, you should respond with either something positive, neutral, or nothing at all. It is human nature to want to give payback when someone wrongs us, but this approach rarely ends well. You are better off if you avoid that kind of response.

If you act calmly during times of conflict, you will not only feel better about yourself, and you will also look better to people who see how you handle the situation. The benefits of taking the high road far outweigh the help you get for your ego if you fight back.

Be careful: I am not saying you should be a pushover or a punching bag for someone. There are times when the only option is to stand up for yourself, or even leave the situation. This probably will not happen very often, however. The goal should be to avoid conflict of any kind unless it cannot be avoided.

*TIP #179: Don't make excuses unless you are asked.

Excuse-making often has the opposite effect of what it is intended to do. Instead of proving that you weren't at fault for whatever unfortunate thing that happened, you often just make yourself look like a whiner.

DO: Learn from your mistakes and failures.

DON'T: Make excuses in public.

Unless someone asks for an explanation, excuses almost always make you look soft. Even if they are 100 percent true, you should not gripe about why someone else is to blame for your mistakes, failures, or even bad luck. It is bad enough to make excuses to someone in private, but if you do it in public, you can really make yourself look weak. The best move in these situations is usually to accept the blame (even if you don't deserve it), or better yet, just leave it alone.

*TIP #180: Avoid fuddy-duddies.

Negative and humorless people are no fun to be around.

DO: Avoid people who are overly serious, critical, and generally negative.

DON'T: Think you can't cut people out of your life who regularly bring you down (or at least see them a lot less).

If you have the choice, think carefully about your choices of friends and who you spend time with. If they bring you down, kick them to the curb, or at least spend less time with them.

This advice can be tricky if the fuddy-duddy person in your life is a family member or a business partner. Sometimes we just can't avoid being around certain people. If you have the choice, though, spend time with people who make your life more enjoyable.

Be careful: This is not to say that negative and humorless people are bad people. I just do not want to be around them. And, of course, if you recognize that YOU are the one being the fuddy-duddy, you might want to consider making some changes!

*TIP #181: Do not be more than five minutes late.

Unless there is an important or job-related reason for being on time to the second, being a few minutes late should not matter.

DO: Do your best to be on time when you say you will be somewhere.

DON'T: Stress out about being a few minutes late in informal situations.

The common argument against being late is that you are disrespecting the people who have to wait for you. This might be true if you carelessly make someone wait for a long period of time, but are a few minutes really that big of a deal?

If someone tries to shame you for being a couple of minutes late, do not think you have to apologize unless you want to. It is just not that significant. This is not to say that you shouldn't even try to be on time when it's possible. Just don't get stressed out about it if you don't show up exactly on time. And if someone does make it a big deal about you being a few minutes late, they are telling you a lot about their personality. They may not be the type of person worth spending time with (see tip #180 "Avoid fuddy-duddys").

*TIP #182: Write down what works for you.

If you are trying to improve your communication and social skills, be sure you do not forget to keep track of the successful strategies you learn.

DO: Keep a record of effective communication and social skills strategies you discover.

DON'T: Assume you are going to remember everything you do that works.

If you are a student of communication and social skills, you may learn a strategy that would help you or others. Do not let it disappear because you forgot to record it somewhere.

Be careful: When I first started studying communication and social skills, I often observed people in social situations to try to figure out some of the "secrets of success." Sometimes I would figure out something that was really effective, only to later forget what I had learned. It did not take too many times of forgetting before I got motivated to start taking notes of the things I was learning. Don't let anything slip away that might be useful for you in the future.

*TIP #183: Avoid talking to strangers in loud places.

If your goal is to meet new people for some reason (to make business connections, get a date, casually chat, etc.), then you are better off avoiding places that are so loud that it is hard to hear anyone talk.

DO: Find places you know are quiet if your goal is to talk to strangers.

DON'T: Try to talk to strangers if you must lean in just to be able to have a conversation.

If you decide to go out with the hope of talking to people you do not know, it would be smart to choose places where it is easy to make casual comments. That means not going anywhere that you have to walk up and yell in someone's ear. When that is your only option for talking to people, you have pretty much eliminated the chance to have a casual conversation with them.

Having to lean in and talk to someone *you know* is awkward enough. Don't make it even harder on yourself by trying to do it with strangers.

*TIP #184: Do not feel like you must be outgoing just because you are known for having good social skills.

Hopefully, if you follow enough of the advice in this book, you will get a reputation for having great social skills. Be careful, though, because this can be both a blessing and a curse.

DO: Act how you want to act in social situations.

DON'T: Feel pressured to act a certain way just because you are known for having great social skills.

Even if you do have great social skills, you should not feel like you have to impress people or behave a certain way in social situations just because you do. The goal should still be to be yourself (see tip #1). This advice really applies no matter your level of social skills—you should never feel pressured to behave a certain way. Decide for yourself how you want to act, and don't worry about showing off your skills for other people.

> Story time: This is something I have had to deal with more and more as I have learned to improve my own social skills. Once I started to get a reputation for having good social skills, people would come up to me at events if I was not talking to someone and say something like "I thought you were supposed to be the communication guy. Why aren't you talking to more people?" or something similar. Having great social skills does not mean you should feel obligated to talk to mingle every second of every event you attend. It just means that you CAN do it when you want to.

*TIP #185: Read as much as you can about communication skills.

It may seem like a simple subject, but there is a lot to learn about communication skills if you truly want to be great at it. You can spend your entire life trying to learn it all and still not know everything.

DO: Be obsessed with learning as much as you can about communication and social skills.

DON'T: Overlook the value of them.

Communication skills are extremely valuable and very much worth studying. They can dramatically help us in both our personal and professional lives if we use them well. The more you learn, the better it is.

*TIP #186: Do not make assumptions about people based on traits they share with someone you don't like.

No two people are exactly alike. Just because someone is similar in some way to a person you know does not mean they will automatically be the same in other ways.

DO: Form your opinions about people based on their own actions.

DON'T: Judge people based on things they do that remind you of someone else.

We have to be careful about connecting the dots and making judgments about people's character that aren't actually true. You should not assume someone is a bad person because they have a random common trait with someone you don't like.

For example, if you dated a guy who treated you badly and who was a big sports fan, that does not mean all sports fans will treat you the same way. If your former business partner who stole from you is from a certain part of the country, that does not mean everyone from that area will also cheat you. These examples sound like silly assumptions to make, but people think this way all the time. You should judge people based on their own actions, not on things that remind you of someone else who had other bad qualities.

Be careful: This does not mean you should take this too far and ignore obvious red flags. If someone shows signs that they are violent or easily angered, for instance, you should probably not overlook those signals. The point of this tip is to avoid judging people based on traits that are not necessarily bad on their own but remind you of someone you don't like.

*TIP #187: Keep your hands away from your face during conversations.

Touching your face a lot can be a sign of nervousness, discomfort, and lack of confidence. Even if those things are not actually true about you, it is still not a good idea to give the impression that they might be.

DO: Avoid touching your face or covering your mouth when you talk to people.

DON'T: Stress out if you accidentally touch your face once or twice and realize you should not be doing it.

Be careful: Like a lot of the "don't" advice in this book, you should not freak out if you accidentally slip up and make this mistake once or twice. This tip is not included to make you obsess about never touching your face, just to try to convince you to try to not make it a habit.

If you have ever seen people who touch their faces a lot in social situations, there is something about it that makes them look nervous, uncomfortable, and even suspicious. Whether you actually are nervous or not does not really matter—it is a good idea to not give people a reason to think you might be. There is something about touching your face or covering your mouth when you talk that sends a signal that something is not right about you.

*TIP #188: Do not sacrifice integrity just to avoid awkwardness.

Trying to avoid an uncomfortable situation is no excuse for being dishonest, rude, or disrespectful to someone.

DO: Avoid awkward situations if it is possible, but not if it means sacrificing your integrity.

DON'T: Lie or "ghost" someone to avoid an awkward situation.

I know that awkwardness can be uncomfortable and unpleasant. Nobody would blame you for trying to avoid it whenever you can. If you have to lie or disappear on someone (ghosting) just to avoid the awkwardness of being honest with them, though, you are not showing much character. Sometimes you just have to be an adult and face difficult situations.

Be careful: While I do feel strongly that it is generally not a good idea to disappear to avoid awkward situations, that does not mean you should never do it. You may find yourself in a difficult or unsafe situation where you feel like you have no choice. That is certainly understandable under those circumstances.

*TIP #189: Think from the perspective of your ninety-year-old self.

Thinking from the perspective of an older version of ourselves can help us appreciate what is important today.

DO: Consider what your ninety-year-old self would think about what you are experiencing today.

DON'T: Obsess over every decision you make out of fear of the long-term effects of it.

I know it may be a little uncomfortable to think long term, but there will be a day for all of us when we take our last breath. It could be today, or it could be eighty years from now. That perspective should help us realize how unimportant a lot of the things are that we worry about.

Thinking from the viewpoint of the end of your life is not meant to be depressing, just a strategy to help you keep things in perspective today. When you are ninety years old, for instance, are you going to care about the little annoyances that bothered you in the moment but were quickly forgotten? Will you have regrets about risks you did not take or the broken relationships that you didn't try to repair? Chances are that most of the small-picture things that bother us now will not matter much at the end of our lives. It is best to focus on the things that really are important, like family, friends, our impact on others, and so on

Be careful: I am not saying that you should be so worried about the long-term effect of everything you do that it either paralyzes your decision-making or makes you not care about anything in the moment. You should obviously not take this too far. It is just a matter of realizing what really matters.

*TIP #190: Try to be likable but don't obsess about being liked.

Being popular is great, but you are going to stress yourself out if you worry too much about it.

DO: Try to have likable traits like character, class, unselfishness, sense of humor, and concern for others.

DON'T: Try to make *everyone* like you.

This may sound like a contradiction, but there is a big difference between trying to have likable qualities and worrying about being liked. When our focus is on how we act instead of what other people think of us, *we* have control over the situation. We choose our behavior and then let people decide for themselves if they like it or not. When our peace of mind depends on our popularity, though, we are at their mercy.

Worrying about being disliked is a waste of energy and time anyway. First of all, you will never be able to relax if you are always wondering about who likes you and who doesn't. And second, there is *nobody* in the world whom everyone likes, so it is pointless to be concerned about the ones who don't. It is just inevitable that some people will not like you no matter what you do. That's life. The sooner you accept this fact, the better.

For every person in the history of the world, there is a certain percentage of people who like them and a certain percentage who do not. Even if you could be the most lovable person of all time, it would be impossible to accomplish being liked by 100 percent of all people. So why worry about the ones who do not like us? If it's going to happen anyway, there is no reason to have anxiety about it.

The best (and most freeing) mindset is to commit to being yourself and being a good person and then letting the chips fall where they may. Hopefully, people will like you when you do that, but even if some do not, so what? Be glad about the ones who do and move on with your life.

*TIP #191: Do not feel like you are stuck at your current level of communication skills.

You may feel like you have no hope of *ever* improving your communication skills. Many people who have dramatically improved once thought the same thing.

DO: Believe that you can improve your social skills, no matter how bad they are.

DON'T: Assume that your public speaking, social skills, and other communication skills are set as they are.

Great communication skills do not come naturally for most people. Many of the ones you see who are "never met a stranger" types were not so good at being sociable at some point in their lives. This should be encouraging to you if you feel like there is no chance that you will ever improve your own skills. The same thing is true for public speaking skills and other kinds of communication abilities as well.

Social skills are like sports skills—we may not be able to become the best in the world at them, but we can definitely be taught how to improve. So, while you may never be able to be the "life of the party" or the best public speaker of all time, it is still very possible that you could get dramatically better.

Story time: When I was in high school, I was an extreme introvert. I did not even go to my prom because it was too big of a social event for me to handle. I remember a high school graduation party that I attended where I just sat in the corner and hoped that nobody would talk to me. I could not even socialize with

people I knew in social settings, much less talk to strangers! And yet I somehow went from that level of social ability to becoming a full-on people person.
I reached a point where I was able to reduce social fear and anxiety to nothing
but small annoyances, if they existed at all. So how did I accomplish this? The
beginning of the process was believing that it was even possible to improve. I
also got serious about committing to getting better. You might think that it is
impossible to improve the communication skills that give you trouble, but I am
here to tell you that it is possible to do it if you are motivated to do so, maybe
even by a lot. I know because I did it.

*TIP #192: Be quick to forgive.

Being unable to forgive is a poison that will hurt you *far* more than it will
hurt the person you are not forgiving.

DO: Forgive people who wrong you for *any* reason.

DON'T: Feel like you must stay in relationships of any kind when you
have been wronged.

I know that this may be tough advice to take because it is not human nature
to forgive people who wrong us. You absolutely must make yourself do it,
though. Holding on to unforgiveness will only make you feel worse in the
long run.

The willingness and ability to forgive others will really help you when it
concerns less serious issues. Can you get over the argument you had with
your spouse this morning? Can you forgive someone for snapping at you
when they were having a bad day? Being able to forgive people quickly for
relatively small matters is one of the main ingredients of keeping both business and personal relationships strong. It may require you to work at it if you
are not used to forgiving so easily, but the benefits are worth it.

*Be careful: It is important that I include this side note with this tip—for-
giveness does not mean the relationship has to stay the same way it was
before you were wronged. If a business partner cheated you out of a lot of
money, for instance, forgiving that person does not require that you stay
partners. Or if you are in a romantic relationship and your partner physically
abuses you, forgiveness does not mean you have to stay with that person. But
it does mean you do not have to carry the burden of holding a grudge for the
rest of your life.*

*TIP #193: Instead of obsessively remembering people who have wronged you, remember people who have been good to you instead.

Holding grudges is a waste of time and energy. It's much better to do the opposite and never forget people who have done something *for* you instead.

DO: Never forget when people do something good for you—and look for opportunities to do something for them to show appreciation.

DON'T: Hold grudges and obsess over getting revenge against people who have wronged you.

Have you ever known someone who holds grudges? Some people hold them for years, even decades. It sticks with them like a pebble in their shoe that they can't get rid of until they give their payback—what a sad, stressful way to live.

Instead of doing that, it's better to keep a mental record of people who have done something *good* for you, waiting for your chance to return the favor. Now that is a better kind of payback!

Never forgetting people who have done good to you will make you stand out because most people do not think like this. It is much better than obsessing about getting revenge, and more fun too.

*TIP #194: Be careful who you listen to for advice.

There are a lot of smart people in the world. Not everyone gives good advice, though.

DO: Seek out advice from smart people you know and trust.

DON'T: Take advice without thinking it through yourself.

Some people seem smart but are not actually very smart at all. Some are book smart but don't really have common sense. Others are good people but do not have much wisdom. It is hard to blame someone for trying to help you by giving advice, but you should always consider the source when that happens. Sometimes people may not know your situation well enough to be able to tell you anything useful, or they may think that something that worked for them will work just as well for you. That is not always the case.

Be careful: Most people will not be able to understand your situation fully. It can sometimes be helpful to listen to advice from your family, friends, and so on, and it doesn't hurt to ask; just realize that their suggestions may not always be your best course of action.

*TIP #195: Be aware that a high percentage of women have been sexually harassed and assaulted.

I do not think a lot of men realize how many women have been sexually harassed or assaulted at some point in their lives and how some may be afraid of that happening to them. Men should be sensitive to the possibility of this when they are in situations where a woman might feel uncomfortable.

DO: Be sensitive to the possibility that a woman you are talking to has been sexually harassed or assaulted.

DON'T: Put a woman in a situation where she might feel trapped or uncomfortable.

This is a heavy subject, but it is an important one. Men are not always great at having empathy or awareness for the unique experiences that women have sometimes been through. Whether you are in a personal or professional setting, always take into consideration the possibility that you may be putting a woman in an uncomfortable situation. Keep that in mind when you are scheduling appointments, having meetings, introducing people, having casual conversations, and so on. You can never go wrong by trying to be considerate of other people's fears and things that might cause them discomfort.

*TIP #196: Be careful how you compliment strangers.

Giving a compliment can be a great way to break the ice with a stranger or spread general positive energy. Just be sure that you do it appropriately.

DO: Look for opportunities to compliment people you do not know.

DON'T: Compliment on things that may come across as flirty, creepy, or weird.

Some earlier tips addressed the importance of breaking the ice to talk to new people, but there needs to be a separate one about the use of compliments. Complimenting strangers is a great thing to do, but it can cause problems if you are not careful about how you go about it. A good general rule for giving compliments to people you do not know is to look for things that obviously stand out. If you see someone wearing a wild-looking, multicolored hat, for instance, it makes sense that a person might comment. The person can't really complain or think you are being awkward if you say something about it. It is common sense that something like that might inspire people to talk.

Strategies to avoid when complimenting strangers are things like (A) complimenting something that is not obviously out of the ordinary or (B) complimenting a physical feature. When you compliment something that is not out of the ordinary, you make it look like you are going out of your way to compliment them. That can come across a little weird. The same goes for complimenting a physical feature. These kinds of comments may give the impression that you are flirting. Unless trying to get a date with someone is actually your goal, you should stay away from anything that might be taken romantically and keep your comments appropriate for the situation.

The impression you should be going for when you give someone a compliment is that you could not help but do it because it stood out so much. That way your comment looks sincere and you won't look like you have some secret motive.

Be careful: Being willing to give people compliments is great; just be aware of the way you give them and to whom you are giving them. I have found that the key to avoiding awkwardness when giving compliments is to be casual about it and use a little discretion about the areas you call attention to.

*TIP #197: Be strategic about how you respond to bullies.

Most people have to deal with a bully at some point in their lives, sometimes even as adults. It is easier to handle them if you have a plan for the situation before it happens.

DO: Have a plan for handling bullies.

DON'T: Try to react to bullies in the moment.

If you try to react to bullies in the moment, you may regret how you respond or do not respond. It is much better when you know what you plan to do about them ahead of time.

You really only have two choices when someone bullies you: You can (1) just take it and say nothing or (2) respond in some way.

1.) Ignoring the person is probably the most common advice for handling bullies, but this strategy can backfire. If you choose to say nothing, yes, there is a chance that it may never happen again, but there is also a possibility that bullies will see this as a free pass to keep doing it. They may also even get angry if they feel disrespected by being ignored. Choosing to do nothing can also make you feel bad about yourself, so be sure you keep these things in mind before you decide to choose this response. You have to read the situation to be able to make a good response.

2.) If you decide to say something back, it is *very* important that you choose your words carefully. The best approach is to react as calmly as possible and to show you are not going to stand for it but also that you are not all that bothered by the bully's actions. You can accomplish this by using humor or dismissive comments or even by teasing the bully back.

Be careful: If you decide that you want to respond more harshly, you risk getting a harsh response in return. You might have an argument or fight on your hands that is worse than the original bullying if you do this. Calm, unemotional, and logical responses are usually the best way to handle bullies.

*TIP #198: Speak up for people who are being bullied.

If you see someone being bullied, you should defend them.

DO: Stand up to people who are bullying others.

DON'T: Do nothing when you see someone being bullied.

Bullying is not just something that takes place in school. It can happen to people of all ages, including adults. No matter how old a person is when it happens to them, bullying can affect self-esteem and even mental health. It is obviously something that should be stopped, and you may be the only chance that a bullied person has to be helped.

Bullying can include everything from simple joking and teasing to aggressively mean behavior. Some forms of it are worse than others, but none of it should be tolerated. This is not to say that you have to lose your temper and get angry when you see someone being bullied, but you should still try to stop it somehow if you can. Sometimes just speaking up is enough. It may even be possible that the bully thinks it is no big deal and does not even realize the effect it is having. No matter what the person's intention is, though, bullying should still never be allowed to happen.

Be careful: I should, of course, give the same warning that I mentioned in my last tip about handling bullying on your own. Just as when you are being bullied yourself, when you take a stand for someone else, you should be prepared for a harsh response. That is why it is usually best to try to handle it calmly and unemotionally if at all possible. Speaking up against a bully can spark anger, especially if you do not handle it well. Sometimes you can put an end to bullying just by casually calling it out and drawing attention to it, and it may even occasionally be possible to stop it with humor. There is no one method that works every time, so try to figure out what response fits the situation best.

*TIP #199: Don't feel like you have to hide your religious beliefs in professional settings.

Your spiritual life is a personal thing. You should not feel obligated to share everything you believe with people, but you also should not think that you have to hide it.

DO: Feel free to be open about your religious beliefs.

DON'T: Be respectful of people who don't believe the same way you do.

If your faith is something that is important to you, you should feel comfortable sharing as much or as little about it as you want. Whether that means putting out a religious quote every now and then on your social media or talking with people about your recent church service, the way that you share your faith should be up to you. If that means keeping it totally private, you can do that too. Just do not think you *have* to hide it.

Be careful: There is a risk, of course, that people who believe differently than you will not want to associate with you or do business with you based on your beliefs. That is a risk that you will have to consider when deciding exactly how much you want to talk about your beliefs and in what way.

*TIP #200: Do not think that communication skills are all-or-nothing traits that people either have or don't have.

Communication and social skills are not abilities that some people are lucky enough to be blessed with and some are not. It's more like a scale than a yes or no trait.

DO: Focus on making small improvements in your communication and social skills.

DON'T: Worry about making drastic improvement quickly.

It is a mistake to think that you can never improve your communication skills. No matter how introverted you are or how anxious you get when talking to people, you have the potential to get better.

If these skills were unchangeable, there would be no reason to try to improve them and nobody would have ever done it before. History is full of famous people who were nervous speakers and later learned how to eliminate or overcome their weaknesses, though.

It is easier to have hope for improvement when you realize that communication and social skills exist on a scale rather than an all-or-nothing situation of good or bad. When you think of these skills this way, making small improvements seems much more manageable. You do not have to feel like the goal is to go from bad to great, but just to move up the scale. That is something everyone can do!

Thankfully "bad" and "good" are not the only possible options when it comes to communication skills. If that were the case, then trying to make the leap from bad to good would be intimidating and nearly impossible. It would be hard to have any hope of ever improving. That is not the case, though. If you are a 2 out of 10 on the scale, moving to a 3 does not seem quite so impossible. It seems way more doable than having to go from bad to good all at once. It might take more work for some people than others, but we are all capable of moving up the scale of communication skills.

Story time: Do not give up if you feel as if your communication and social skills are not as good as you wish they were. They don't have to stay that way. Making drastic improvements is a part of my story, so I know it can be done. No matter what your current ability or anxiety level is in any communication-dependent situation, you can do it too.

Conclusion

There you have it. Those are the 200 communication skills commandments that I would urgently tell my eighteen-year-old self if I could. How awesome would it be if I could actually give this book to that guy, or even to the twenty-eight-year-old me. It would have saved me a *lot* of awkwardness, discomfort, failures, and missed opportunities. I do not feel bad that I missed out, though, because learning these lessons was part of my growth process. The character development that I experienced enabled me to get where I am today.

I wrote this book to save you the time and struggle it took me to learn all this information. Hopefully, you will be able to use it to transform yourself into a more confident, comfortable, less anxious, and successful communicator in personal and professional situations of all kinds.

If I could do it, so can you.

Appendix

The Tips

CHAPTER 1. SOCIAL COMFORT: OVERCOMING SOCIAL ANXIETY

*TIP #1: Be you and don't apologize for it.

*TIP #2: Be authentic in all social situations.

*TIP #3: Keep a healthy perspective by having a "no agenda" mindset when talking to strangers.

*TIP #4: Count your blessings.

*TIP #5: Talk to people wherever you go to build comfort in social situations.

*TIP #6: Don't fear awkwardness.

*TIP #7: Get enough sleep.

*TIP #8: Do not worry about things that are beyond your control.

*TIP #9: Coach yourself during times of anxiety.

*TIP #10: Do not think about the white elephant to try to overcome negative thoughts.

*TIP #11: Act confident.

*TIP #12: Overcome "intimidating person" anxiety by valuing everyone highly.

*TIP #13: Stay calm under pressure.

*TIP #14: Do not overvalue the significance of stressful situations.

*TIP #15: Don't rely on liquid courage to overcome social anxiety.

*TIP #16: If all else fails in your fight against social anxiety, act like you are playing a part in a play of someone who is not anxious.

*TIP #17: Connect your mindset in situations where you have no anxiety to ones where you do.

CHAPTER 2. LIKABILITY

*TIP #18: Be positive.

*TIP #19: Don't be a sugar blower.

*TIP #20: Don't be a try-hard.

*TIP #21: Do not get into arguments or heated debates over insignificant things.

*TIP #22: Try to avoid acting desperate in social situations.

*TIP #23: Make kindness a habit.

*TIP #24: Don't brag.

*TIP #25: Don't gossip.

*TIP #26: Don't be nosey.

*TIP #27: Don't be a busybody.

*TIP #28: Be obsessively dependable.

*TIP #29: Be careful about telling people "I told you so."

*TIP #30. Do not break plans with people casually.

*TIP #31: Be considerate of others (and say "thank you" when people are considerate of you).

*TIP #32: Eliminate the phrase "shut up" from your life.

*TIP #33: Do not get mad at people who don't follow your advice after they ask for it.

*TIP #34: Make a commitment to remembering and using people's names.

*TIP #35: Keep your car clean.

*TIP #36: Have good posture.

*TIP #37: Don't "ghost" when you are not interested in talking to someone.

*TIP #38: Don't tell everyone about your problems (in person or online).

*TIP #39: Be careful about using people's words against them.

*TIP #40: Do not try too hard to be cool.

*TIP #41: Be decisive.

*TIP #42: Do not be clingy with people you know during social situations.

*TIP #43: Slow down (speaking and movements).

*TIP #44: Overcome the fear of embarrassment.

*TIP #45: Answer personal emails, texts, calls, and so on quickly.

*TIP #46: Don't cry over spilled milk.

*TIP #47: Treat people you meet as if they are already friends.

*TIP #48: Smile when you greet people.

*TIP #49: Be careful who you tease and how.

*TIP #50: Do not automatically assume something is wrong with you if some people do not like you.

*TIP #51: Do not act as if you are in charge if you do not have the authority to be.

*TIP #52: Be careful how you use sarcasm.

*TIP #53: Never tell someone to "calm down."

*TIP #54: Wash your hands after you go to the bathroom.

*TIP #55: Don't be obsessively competitive.

*TIP #56: Don't be an over-apologizer.

CHAPTER 3. CHARACTER ISSUES

Integrity

*TIP #57: Be obsessed with doing what you say you are going to do.

*TIP #58: Don't use NO ANSWER as your "NO" answer.

*TIP #59: Always choose the classy move.

*TIP #60: Do not be afraid to admit your mistakes.

Manners

*TIP #61: Be aware of other people's personal space.

*TIP #62: Learn from old people.

*TIP #63: Show gratitude for compliments (even if you disagree with them).

*TIP #64: Say "excuse me" if you bump into someone.

Doing Good

*TIP #65: Use your money to spread positivity.

*TIP #66: Tip waitstaff one more dollar than what feels like the right amount.

*TIP #67: Do random acts of kindness.

*TIP #68: Share what you learn about communication skills with others.

CHAPTER 4. CONVERSATIONS

Starting Conversations

*TIP #69: Do not be afraid to talk to strangers.

*TIP #70: Memorize a few icebreaker phrases.

*TIP #71: Look for obvious reasons to make icebreaking comments to strangers.

*TIP #72: Master the throwaway comment.

*TIP #73: Be open to having strangers start conversations with you.

*TIP #74: Wear unusual things that might inspire others to start a conversation with you.

*TIP #75: Do not start a conversation with a stranger in an awkward way.

*TIP #76: Don't be afraid of looking like you are hitting on strangers if you talk to them.

Middle of Conversations

*TIP #77: Be totally focused on the person you are talking to.

*TIP #78: Do not act like you are giving a job interview when you talk to people you just met.

*TIP #79: Tell stories during conversations.

*TIP #80: Look for something in common to talk about with people you just met.

*TIP #81: Don't be weird about eye contact.

*TIP #82: Be aware of other people's comfort level during conversations.

*TIP #83: Don't interrupt people during conversations unless you have a really good reason.

*TIP #84: Do not ignore the group when you approach a stranger who is already talking to other people.

Ending Conversations

*TIP #85: Don't wait for the other person to end your conversation if you are ready to stop talking.

*TIP #86: Use transitions to end conversations smoothly.

*TIP #87: Don't make up fake reasons to leave conversations.

CHAPTER 5. ON THE PHONE
(CALLING, TEXTING, ETC.)

*TIP #88: Text like you talk.

*TIP #89: Have good phone manners.

*TIP #90: Act like you are glad to talk to people on the phone.

*TIP #91: Don't send a million text messages to someone without being answered.

*TIP #92: Proofread texts (and other written messages) before you send them.

CHAPTER 6. SOCIAL MEDIA WISDOM

*TIP #93: Avoid saying anything digitally that you would not want to be made public.

*TIP #94: Do not complain about your friends or your significant other on social media.

*TIP #95: Do not share too much of your personal business on social media.

*TIP #96: Don't "like," retweet, comment, or share things on other people's social media at 3 a.m.

*TIP #97: Try to answer every single person who comments on your social media posts.

CHAPTER 7. GENERAL COMMUNICATION
AND SOCIAL SKILLS AT WORK

*TIP #98: Respect authority unless given a reason not to.

*TIP #99: Do not publicly insult your coworkers.

*TIP #100: Don't complain publicly about your boss.

*TIP #101: Return work emails, calls, and texts ASAP.

*TIP #102: Follow the karma business strategy.

*TIP #103: Be careful about talking about sensitive subjects like politics, religion, and even sports at work.

*TIP #104: Do not tell inappropriate jokes at work.

*TIP #105: Always follow through with your promises at work (big and small).

*TIP #106: Go above and beyond with customer service.

*TIP #107: Don't believe the idea that you have to be dishonest to be successful in business.

*TIP #108: Do not break or change plans for meetings with professional contacts if at all possible.

*TIP #109: Smile and be friendly when you work with the public, even if you are in a bad mood.

*TIP #110: Don't complain about your problems (personal or professional) when you are around customers.

*TIP #111: Do not wear sunglasses when you meet with people you don't know well.

*TIP #112: Always have great phone manners at work.

*TIP #113: Don't be afraid to cold call, cold email, or cold DM.

*TIP #114: Do not be dishonest in any way at work (not even white lies).

*TIP #115: Don't drink too much coffee, soda, or alcohol before professional events.

*TIP #116: Use good grammar in professional situations.

CHAPTER 8. LEADERSHIP

*TIP #117: Overcommunicate your expectations when you are in a leadership position.

*TIP #118: Use both praise and criticism when you are in a position of leadership.

*TIP #119: Don't act like a know-it-all.

*TIP #120: Be unemotional when you discipline.

CHAPTER 9. PUBLIC SPEAKING

*TIP #121: Commit to being yourself when you give a presentation or speech.

*TIP #122: Overprepare for speeches and presentations.

*TIP #123: Have a hard beginning and hard ending when public speaking.

*TIP #124: Always try to end your presentations ON TIME.

*TIP #125: Don't admit to being nervous during a speech.

*TIP #126: Be interesting, entertaining, or dramatic—if you can't be any of those things, be brief.

*TIP #127: Make eye contact with your audience.

*TIP #128: Involve the audience when you are public speaking, if possible.

*TIP #129: Do not overvalue the importance of your presentations.

*TIP #130: Do not mumble when public speaking.

*TIP #131: Do not chew gum when giving a speech.

*TIP #132: Don't get obsessed worrying about saying space filler words like "uh," "um," and "you know."

*TIP #133: Smile at your audience at the beginning of your presentations.

*TIP #134: Don't assume your audience thinks your content is as interesting as you do.

*TIP #135: Don't depend on your slides during a presentation.

*TIP #136: Do not make presentations in professional situations the same way you did when you were in school.

CHAPTER 10. COMMUNICATION AND SOCIAL SKILLS FOR YOUR JOB SEARCH

*TIP #137: Do not wait for jobs to be advertised before you ask about openings.

*TIP #138: Be friendly during job interviews.

*TIP #139: During job interviews, calm your nerves by having a mindset that you are interviewing them too.

CHAPTER 11. NETWORKING

Networking Events

*TIP #140: Do not stay with one person for more than a few minutes at networking events.

*TIP #141: Move on from conversations when there is no interest or connection at networking events.

*TIP #142: If networking and other business events might help you, go to them even when you do not feel like it.

*TIP #143: Dress well for networking events but not TOO well.

*TIP #144: Take steps to fight bad breath at networking events.

*TIP #145: Do not think of every interaction as pass/fail at networking events.

*TIP #146: Pretend that you are already friends with everyone you meet at networking events.

*TIP #147: Don't be afraid to approach any size group of people at networking events.

*TIP #148: Don't automatically avoid networking events with high ticket prices.

*TIP #149: Do not smother people at networking events.

*TIP #150: Don't take too much time talking to people you already know at networking events.

*TIP #151: If networking events cause you extreme anxiety, go somewhere on your way to them to talk to a stranger to warm up.

*TIP #152: Do not flirt or joke inappropriately at business events.

*TIP #153: Take no for an answer at networking events.

*TIP #154: Do not be afraid to stand alone at networking events.

*TIP #155: Do not avoid networking events where you do not seem to fit in.

*TIP #156: Do not make assumptions about networking events and the people who attend them.

*TIP #157: Have big picture goals at networking events.

Random Networking

*TIP #158: Always be ready to give your thirty-second pitch.

*TIP #159: Do not give your business card out immediately when meeting someone new.

*TIP #160: Be aware of people's body language and other signals when you are networking (just don't over read it).

*TIP #161: Be memorable when making a first impression.

*TIP #162: Send a message within twenty-four hours of getting contact info when you are networking.

*TIP #163: Make introductions to help others connect.

*TIP #164: Get advice from older, experienced networkers about their methods.

*TIP #165: Try to get to the phrase "what do you do?" as quickly as possible when networking.

*TIP #166: Don't wait for official networking events to network.

CHAPTER 12. GENERAL COMMUNICATION AND SOCIAL SKILLS WISDOM

*TIP #167: Be obsessed with self-awareness.

*TIP #168. Don't judge people too harshly for bad behavior if their intent is good.

*TIP #169: Do not compare yourself to others.

*TIP #170: Don't be embarrassed to go out solo.

*TIP #171: Be intentional about establishing a good reputation.

*TIP #172: Regularly look for opportunities to sharpen your communication and social skills.

*TIP #173: Give a good handshake.

*TIP #174: Do not feel obligated to explain why you can't make plans with someone.

*TIP #175: Be careful about drawing conclusions from people's words and actions.

*TIP #176: Don't walk with your head down.

*TIP #177: Don't be an "eye-contact-avoiding zombie."

*TIP #178: Take the high road as much as possible.

*TIP #179: Don't make excuses unless you are asked.

*TIP #180: Avoid fuddy-duddies.

*TIP #181: Do not be more than five minutes late.

*TIP #182: Write down what works for you.

*TIP #183: Avoid talking to strangers in loud places.

*TIP #184: Do not feel like you must be outgoing just because you are known for having good social skills.

*TIP #185: Read as much as you can about communication skills.

*TIP #186: Do not make assumptions about people based on traits they share with someone you don't like.

*TIP #187: Keep your hands away from your face during conversations.

*TIP #188: Do not sacrifice integrity just to avoid awkwardness.

*TIP #189: Think from the perspective of your ninety-year-old self.

*TIP #190: Try to be likable but don't obsess about being liked.

*TIP #191: Do not feel like you are stuck at your current level of communication skills.

*TIP #192: Be quick to forgive.

*TIP #193: Instead of obsessively remembering people who have wronged you, remember people who have been good to you instead.

*TIP #194: Be careful who you listen to for advice.

*TIP #195: Be aware that a high percentage of women have been sexually harassed and assaulted.

*TIP #196: Be careful how you compliment strangers.

*TIP #197: Be strategic about how you respond to bullies.

*TIP #198: Speak up for people who are being bullied.

*TIP #199: Don't feel like you have to hide your religious beliefs in professional settings.

*TIP #200: Do not think that communication skills are all-or-nothing traits that people either have or don't have.